D0204665

THE GIRL IN THE BACK

THE GIRL IN THE BACK

A FEMALE DRUMMER'S LIFE
with BOWIE, BLONDIE,
and the '70S ROCK SCENE

LAURA DAVIS-CHANIN

An Imprint of Hal Leonard LLC

Published in 2018 by Backbeat Books
An Imprint of Hal Leonard LLC
7777 West Bluemound Road
Milwaukee, WI 53213

Trade Book Division Editorial Offices
33 Plymouth St., Montclair, NJ 07042

Every reasonable effort has been made to contact copyright holders and secure permissions. Omissions can be remedied in future editions.

Book design by Kristina Rolander

Printed in the United States of America

Library of Congress Cataloging-in-Publication Data is available upon request.

ISBN 978-1-61713-687-0

www.backbeatbooks.com

To Bill Arning; Philip Shelley; David Scharff; Lori Reese;
Joe Katz; Jody Robelo Katz; Antone DeSantis; Paul Rutner;
MB Davis; my exquisite daughters, Zoe and Mara;
and the Man Who Fell to Earth,
may he rest in peace

CONTENTS

FOREWORD

THE STUDENT TEACHERS WAS THE FIRST band I ever saw that had a female drummer.

Laura and I, along with Bill Arning, who was also in the Student Teachers, went to the same high school in New York City in the mid-to-late '70s. At first, I was not really friends with them, but it was a small school, so I was aware of them forming a band, running the fan club for the Mumps, and being into "New Wave." Bill was an especially vocal Mumps devotee and hippie denouncer. I remember him constantly yelling out "Deadhead!" at me in the hallways, having once spotted a copy of *Blues for Allah* in my locker from way across the common room in our school. I was not a Deadhead, more of a Dead-dabbler, and not for long. Years later, I suspiciously wondered how he was able to recognize this fairly muted Grateful Dead album cover from so far away. Bill always had a keen eye for art!

Pretty soon I was a fan of the Mumps myself. I got to know Laura's sister, MB, and we'd go see them and the Student Teachers, as well as Blondie, the Heartbreakers, and lots of other bands mentioned in the book. MB and I became close friends, and I even ended up working for her and Laura's father and stepmother at their loft one summer, and later moved in there with MB when they went to Europe for a few months. But earlier in our friendship, when I tagged along with MB to see the Student Teachers, I remember being impressed that they had a female rhythm section. I don't know if I was already thinking about playing drums then, but I definitely took notice of Laura, with her methodical non-splashy drumming and androgynous coolness! She certainly *was* cool, if not a bit intimidating. And her willful personality came through from behind the drums, despite being in the back.

Now that I think about it, I'm pretty sure it was Laura (and later on, Moe Tucker) who inspired me to play the drums. I recognize that same intensity and passion in Laura's description of her youth and extraordinary experiences that I saw when she performed. She recounts stories so vividly. It's as though she's transcribing a diary. I was completely swept up in the emotion of it, both from reading about all the events I recall, when I hung out with MB, and the ones that were new to me.

Georgia Hubley
Drummer, Yo La Tengo
January 2018

ACKNOWLEDGMENTS

I FIRST WANT TO THANK MY AGENT, Lee Sobel, for pushing me to write this book. Despite my initial hesitation, it was very cathartic. I next want to thank my dear friend and editor Paul Rutner for helping me so much in the writing of this book and, even more important, for making me laugh through it all. Of course I want to thank Chris Stein for his wonderful thoughts and encouragement. I am also grateful to my band, the Student Teachers: Bill Arning, Lori Reese, David Scharff, Philip Shelley, Jody Robelo Katz, Joe Katz, and Antone DeSantis. They were so supportive, and despite my annoying, endless questions about things that happened, who, why, how, where—they weathered me with great patience. It's also important to say that without these exceptional people, my life then— and the roller-coaster ride of events that happened to me and to all of us—would never have occurred. I want to thank Roberta Bayley, David Godlis, Bobby Grossman, Joe Stevens, Ebet Roberts, Bill Arning, Gary Valentine, Lisa Jane Persky, Chris Stein, and particularly Steve Lombardi for their beautiful photos, which bring this book to life far more than it ever would otherwise. We are all so lucky these photographers were there to capture that unique, bristling moment in rock 'n' roll history. I'd like to thank my acquiring editor, Bernadette Malavarca, along with group publisher John Cerullo, at Backbeat Books for seeing an important story to tell here. Thanks also to copy editor Polly Watson and designer Kristina Rolander. Finally, I want to thank my sister, MB, for being my rock; to Chris A., for being there; and to my remarkable daughters, Zoe and Mara. I am a far better person because of them.

INTRODUCTION

WAIT! HOLD IT! JUST HOLD IT! I want to tell you something first. That is: this is not the book you think it is. Yes, it's a memoir—yes, yes, it will tell you about a lot of cool people and places I got to meet and go to and yes, it will tell you about how it all fell apart.

But . . . it's not a sad story.

And that's very important to remember. You know, this Greek philosopher, Heraclitus—well, he said many wild and complicated things, but the most famous was:

No man ever steps in the same river twice.

That's the point of this book. Life happens fast. The changes it hits us with every day are stupefying. Nothing remains the same. That reality was highly concentrated for me, for all of us, during the span covered in this book, because my friends and I were in our teen years then—a classically dangerous time for anyone—and it all happened during a unique moment in rock 'n' roll history. The river we were stepping in was thunderous.

During the late '70s in New York, music was transforming every minute of every day right before our eyes. Gone were the big stadium acts and in came Punk Rock—the queen of the rock revolution—embodied by small, angry, individualistic bands who demanded to be heard and recognized, and my friends and me—we jumped right smack into the middle of that revolution, just as the river was raging. It grabbed us by our necks and took us with it. As Patti Smith said:

To me, punk rock is the freedom to create, freedom to be successful, freedom to not be successful, freedom to be who you are. It's freedom.[1]

And honestly—we were a little too young for that freedom.

Two years ago, I was approached by my agent to write this book. I was in the middle of working on another one, so I hesitated. But he contacted me because David Bowie had just died. He knew about my past friendship

---

1   Sarah Nicole Prickett, "Patti Smith: The Responsible Artist," *Globe and Mail*, June 11, 2012, http://www.theglobeandmail.com/arts/music/patti-smith-the-responsible-artist/article4249178/.

with Bowie and the effect he'd had on my life. He also knew about my relationship with Jimmy Destri of Blondie, and about the production work Jimmy had done for the band I was in, the Student Teachers, and that it had looked at one time, in the late '70s, like our band was getting very successful very quickly.

Until we didn't.

I had actively said to myself a few times through the years that I would never tell this story. Why? Maybe because as exciting and unspeakably remarkable that time was for me and our band, it was also extremely painful. I had to grow up very fast, and, as I was doing that, I was hit smack in the face in 1980—by multiple sclerosis.

But you and I know that as we are hiking the mountain range of this life, we are all kicked in the gut by many things. And honestly, I was lucky. Lucky to have been stopped when I was, because rock 'n' roll, despite the glamour, the fun, the money, was not an easy life. Many of us were really young at that time, and there were a lot of drugs. It felt like it was getting dangerous and, even scarier, possibly fatal.

It all started, as you will see, with the band that my friends and I formed in 1978—the Student Teachers. Even though we were all teenagers and most of us were still in high school, punk rock in downtown New York City seduced us. My friends and I found each other at Patti Smith poetry readings, Jonathan Richman concerts, early Ramones, Blondie, and Talking Heads gigs in the exploding clubs CBGB and Max's Kansas City. These clubs also featured bands such as the Dead Boys, the Heartbreakers, Richard Hell & the Voidoids, Television, the Cramps, the Erasers, the Fast, the Mumps, and so many more. It seized us.

And, as thrilled as I was to jump into that world, I was still a high school student, which generally wouldn't matter, except that I adored academics. That struggle between my studies and rock 'n' roll became a never-ending battle for my soul at that time.

Jimmy Destri ended up producing our debut single for Ork Records and two cuts on the compilation album *Marty Thau Presents 2X5*. Even more provocatively, he became interested in me, which led me on a whirlwind experience with Blondie and, astonishingly, David Bowie. Bowie developed an interest in our band, led us into new territories, and shepherded us through complicated decisions, which, curiously and unfortunately, contributed to us not signing with RCA Records in 1979. Finally, it was Bowie's intelligence and influence that pushed me to go where I really wanted to go—very far from rock 'n' roll.

But back to the story—I became the drummer of our band not because I had always wanted to be a drummer, or even a musician, but because it seemed like a great thing to do at that time. We all thought it was a terrific idea, a key move during a revolutionary time in rock 'n' roll. Female drummers were unusual in the late '70s. Girls were usually in the front.

Not in the back.

THE GIRL IN THE BACK

PART 1

1

THE MAN WHO FELL TO EARTH

IT WAS COLOSSAL. The dark ceilings disappeared within themselves against the titanic space around them. When I entered, I was so far in the back that I felt like an ant. I just stood there watching the entire stadium, filled with fans leaping into the heavens above them with their swinging lighted glow sticks, tossing their drinks all around them, vibrating madly in anticipation, waiting in dreaminess: They were exuberant at being here, at seeing him—small, dancing kernels of mania about to explode. It was 1976 at Madison Square Garden in New York City, and my heart was blasting through my chest.

I gulped a gallon of saliva and quickly ran up behind Bill, my best friend from high school. He was looking for our seats. When we finally found them, farther back, up a sheet of steps into the stratosphere of the arena, I teetered on the edge, panting, and eyeing the stage, looking for him. Bill sat back and sipped his Pepsi. He had done this dozens of times. Not me. This was my first concert. I was fourteen. And it was him.

Thirty minutes later, the stage exploded. The Thin White Duke— David Bowie—ran on and immediately broke into "Station to Station." Bill and I jumped into the night above us, dancing and screaming and crying out to him. The Man Who Fell to Earth. He captivated the entire arena. He electrified each one of us. He quickly dove into "Suffragette City," and, as the lights streamed across the stage, brightening him and lifting him, I fell back down into my seat, staring in awe. Of course, he seized my teenage heart. But it was much more than that. And, to me, he became much more than just a distant star.

2

THREE YEARS LATER

THE SWEAT SCARED ME. I'd never sweated like that before in my life. It was drowning me, and I stunk. I smelled ghastly. Maybe it was my incessant jittering that was making me swelter—bouncing back and forth, back and forth, waiting behind that curtain to go onstage. Bouncing, bouncing. My sticks were covered in the sweat slipping down my fists. Jody handed me a towel. I wiped them while listening to the crowd murmur excitedly in the theater, out front. That just made it worse. I wiped my hands on my thighs. The stage lights were dark, in preparation. Techies dashed madly back and forth, cooking the overheads. I eyed them, wiping the sweat off my lip. I handed the towel back to Jody and returned to bouncing. I looked at the guys. David, a Mick Jagger look-alike, had the endless front-man energy, and he was hot then. But right now, he wasn't sweating torrents of panic, like I was. Bill, the keyboardist, paced around, but he always did that, smiling at it all. Lori, holding her bass, motioned through the riff of our first song, and Philip, the broken soul of us all, took a swig of scotch, shoved the bottle back in his pocket, and ran his hand down the neck of his Stratocaster. They were game for this. Suddenly the stage lights flashed on. My hair was dark with sweat. Jody ushered us onstage as I grabbed the towel from her again. I mashed my hair dry, following the rest of the band, and ran to my drums. I didn't know why I was so freaked. We had been here—going onstage—so many times in the last year. Except . . . tonight was different.

Quickly, the show became a fiasco. After we started banging out our signature song, "Christmas Weather," I lost all sound. I couldn't hear the other instruments at all. I looked frantically over to Lori and Bill, but I could barely see them. The above stage lights slammed us so bright and hot, I was sure they were somehow muffling the sound from the speakers. All I could do was keep the beat I had memorized from rehearsals and gigs, and pray the others were playing in time with me. But when I heard shouts from the audience—"Get off!"—I knew we weren't quite making it. We were all having trouble hearing each other, even though the stage monitors had been fine during rehearsal. When the show finally ended and we ran offstage, our fans—seated close in the first few rows—screamed madly for us, but the rest of the theater filled with boos and empty clapping. This was our peak show. We were opening for Iggy Pop. And it had been set up for us—by David Bowie.

You see, we were merely a group of teenagers who found ourselves dancing through the downtown night club scene in 1978 New York City, drinking White Russians, bonding with embryonic punk rockers and the bursting rock 'n' roll business world on top of us. We met each other in the back of CBGB and Max's Kansas City, and, though we were just out to have fun as fans, we became more than that to each other—a group of exiles, a band, a family. We called ourselves the Student Teachers: David Scharff, the singer; Philip Shelley, the guitar player; Lori Reese, the bass player; Joe Katz on rhythm guitar; Bill Arning, the keyboardist; Jody Robelo, manager; Antone DeSantis, roadie—and me, Laura Davis, the drummer—the girl in the back.

I was seventeen, and this is how I got there.

3

IT STARTED IN BERLIN

THERE ARE TIMES WHEN WE ALL DREAM of meeting our heroes, of making a connection with them, of knowing them, loving them, just being near them. There is no more vital a time when those castles in the air are built than when we're fifteen years old. That was me at fifteen—tireless castle builder.

In the spring of 1977, I spent all my time fantasizing. We were living in Berlin because my father, Douglas Davis, who, besides being the art critic for *Newsweek* magazine and the author of *Art and the Future*, was a performance artist as well. He also videotaped a lot of his work—at the time, video was a new and revolutionary art form. He was on a visiting-artist grant to create, perform, and teach while in residence in Berlin in advance of Documenta 6, which was to be held in Kassel, Germany, and he took us with him.

Divorced from my mom for years, and now with my stepmother, Jane, a beautiful blonde brainiac only ten years older than myself, my dad moved us from New York to the center of Germany for six months, right in the middle of my sophomore year in high school, and before we left, he insisted we read *Mein Kampf* by Adolf Hitler. I'm not sure why he wanted us to do that, because it didn't make me want to go to Berlin any more than when he first announced his plans. Perhaps he thought that by raising our consciousness and knowledge about the man who'd created such incomprehensible ruin in his own country that we would want to understand and learn more when we moved there. He was wrong.

The first thing that happened to me in Berlin was that I developed a chronic sinus infection. I couldn't breathe for the first month. The German air was musty and heavy, carrying, I believed, the weight of its shattered history through every flying particle. I was sure the dark shroud hanging over the country was infecting me.

We ended up staying in a large, colorless, sparsely furnished apartment two blocks from Berlin's Kurfürstendamm, the city's main thoroughfare. The walls were bare and worn-out. There were two shabby chairs and a sofa in the living room that were a tangy blue and nearly fifty years old. I wondered if anyone had ever been in that apartment. What dug at me was not only how big the place was but how desolate and creepy it was, despite the furniture and the refrigerator filled with milk and food—left there by the staff of the university hosting us.

The only windows in the entire place were ceiling-high and out of proportion to the rest of the building. In fact, every bit of the apartment was out of proportion—to itself and to any space around there that made sense. I was chilled by it all. I wondered if that desolate color everywhere was just the way Berlin was then, thirty years after Hitler's suicide—dead dust and stagnation because the Germans hadn't recovered yet. Unfortunately, that dank, dispiriting air hovering outside the giant bedroom windows that MB and I shared just exhausted us.

Honestly, I would have stayed in bed in that fusty Berlin apartment for the entire six months, and so would MB, if Dad hadn't kicked us out of the house every single day when we weren't in school. I doubt he was concerned with us getting out and absorbing the city, meeting people and learning about it all; rather, he needed to work. He always needed to work. And we were constantly in his way.

We attended the high school on the American military base, a short metro ride outside the city. Since we were installed there late in the school year, we made no friends, so we kept close to each other. Every day after school we took the metro back to the Kurfürstendamm and settled in at the only American restaurant on the strip—Burger King. We bought Whoppers and sat down in our usual booth to eat what we knew. It wasn't that German food—sausages sold on the street, or the German pizzas eaten with a knife and fork, or their stews with potatoes and sauerkraut—was bad: It just wasn't home. We munched eagerly, our mouths watering through the burger buns—our small slice of America. Afterward, we usually walked aimlessly down the Kurfürstendamm, peering into the German department stores and shops. Sometimes we sat on a bench near an U-Bahn station and watched the Berliners race home or to work. We never talked much. We were too busy protecting ourselves.

My salvation? My portable cassette recorder. I had packed a black Panasonic tape recorder with tapes I had made of the few bands I was allowed to see in the clubs in New York in 1976. I'd only been to two or three shows because my dad didn't approve of my going. But those few times when Bill and I saw bands at CBGB or Max's Kansas City, and the odd show at City College, I always brought my tape recorder and recorded the band. In Berlin, that tape recorder guarded me and sustained me. It was my water.

Without stopping, unless I was forced to, I listened to the Mumps, Talking Heads, the Ramones, the Dead Boys, Blondie—all live at those clubs—long before they hit it big. More than anything, listening to "Rip Her to Shreds" or "Dance Tunes for the Underdogs" or "Hey Little Girl" or "Blitzkrieg Bop" kept me centered on going home, focused on the idea that there was someplace I would go back to, that I wasn't stuck in that wretched, damaged country forever, that I would return to New York and the music.

Of course, the songs and the music distracted me from the unhappiness I lived in every day but, more than that, they gave me hope. I think that's what a lot of us on the punk scene in the '70s felt at that time. Despite the chains, the blue hair, and the furious lyrics, there was hope. It was a different kind of hope, though—it was more of a revolt. The pent-up feelings of struggle within our communities, in London and New York and in other parts of the UK and U.S.—whether born of financial poverty, social poverty, or artistic poverty—spawned in us a need to express ourselves differently, and that need was developing into a new kind of promise on the music scene. It was a violent hope.

Yet we all loved the Rolling Stones, the Who, the Beatles, the Kinks. But the bands on my tape recorder weren't on the cover of any magazine, or on the record charts and headlining stadiums. I had those tapes because I'd recorded their music sitting five feet away from them at CBGB. They were mine.

And yet, there still was in some bizarre, otherworldly, cryptic, and inexpressible way that same link to Bowie. Yes, he was one of those big stadium acts.

But he also wasn't.

As remote and untouchable as he'd seemed at the Madison Square Garden show the previous year, he wasn't—not to me. He wasn't that distant. Not to me. Even more poignant, and foretelling in its own way, my cassette of Bowie's *Station to Station* was my oxygen. My green leaf in the rain. Lying in that malodorous Berlin bed listening to "Golden Years" and "Word on a Wing," I was with him, close to him as he sang to me, only me, and my fifteen-year-old thirst. Very, very close.

I listened to all those bands when I was in bed, when I woke up, when I was in the shower, on my way to school, on my way back—constantly. I remember that whenever I pressed play without putting on my headphones, Dad was right on me to shut that noise off. He could've been ten miles away: He would immediately descend on my tape recorder, hit the stop button, and scream. He had to work.

Those bands carried me through Berlin and Germany and France, then home, while I swam inside that confused teenage world, facing realities I was nowhere near prepared to understand.

MB and I eventually made friends with a few of my dad's students who, I believe, he sent around to keep an eye on us. Yet they were nice enough. They took us around Berlin to visit museums and restaurants and to see the tourist sights. My father had his art studio in a building situated right in front of the Berlin Wall between East and West Germany—a fifteen-foot-tall, eight-foot-wide mass of reinforced concrete that was topped with an enormous pipe and barbed wire that made climbing over it nearly impossible. We didn't realize what any of that meant until one day he took us up to the roof of the building, and I looked over at the wall and saw one of the East German soldiers, in the guard tower, holding an Uzi.

We still visited East Berlin a few times with his students. The most striking thing about that part of the city was the endless broken walls and torn-down buildings. The city was still riddled with bullet holes, everywhere, from World War II. It was haunting, seeing the level of loss and destruction that I had only read about at school. Even worse, there was never any sun. Never. The world in Berlin was constantly dreary.

One time, Dad's students took us to a documentary at a movie theater on the Kurfürstendamm. It was titled *Hitler: A Career*. This movie was different because it showed rare, never-before-seen film clips about Hitler. My dad's students were young and liberal and free-thinking, and they wanted to see the seeds of their ruined city. I don't think they were planning a revolt. I think they were too devastated. It was beyond unnerving sitting in the middle of this theater watching newsreels of Jewish refugees being tossed into open graves before being methodically shot by Hitler's militia. I remember looking around me, more than at the film. I studied those German faces and eyes, some young, some old, watching what that madman had done in the name of their country. I started getting really nervous. Did I think they might storm the screen in anger, or worse, storm each other, with me and MB in the middle? It was a deeply disturbing experience in a very broken part of the world.

After school ended, we were free. Well, at least we were free from the icy feelings of being unwanted at that American military school, of being the bitter cough medicine everyone was forced to take every day. Then, in the middle of the summer, Dad had to go to Kassel and set up his performance to be broadcast in Documenta 6, so he arranged for us to meet a high school friend of ours in Paris. Paris! We were thrilled, even more so because we would travel there by ourselves: no parents, no adults—just us.

We went to Paris by train, and because we were just fourteen and fifteen years old, and because West Berlin in 1977 was still surrounded by East Berlin and the wall, traveling through there was precarious and scary. Austere East Berlin officers marched through the train performing regular security checks every hour. When the officers knocked on the door to our cabin, the sound was always loud and abrasive. MB and I would jump up and throw our bags under our seats, sure we had something to hide, except there was nothing to hide, other than our ages. We would dutifully hand over our passports and stand at attention—army privates presenting ourselves for inspection. But the soldiers weren't rocked by our young ages when they checked our passports; they were only interested in defectors. That's the way it was everywhere—the clubs in Berlin and Paris and New York. It didn't matter that we were young teens. We were expected to take care of ourselves. And that suited my dad very well. He had his work to do, and he had no time to raise children. No time.

• • •

IN AUGUST, MB AND I FLEW BACK TO THE U.S. by ourselves. We first visited our mother in Virginia, then took the train home to New York. A lot of our lives were spent existing on that Amtrak train between New York and Washington.

We lived with Dad in a loft in SoHo during the shattered late 1970s. The neighborhood consisted largely of old warehouse buildings—many being converted by daring young artists for living and creating paintings, sculpture, performance art, and videos. Although it eventually evolved into the mecca of the downtown art scene, at that time, it was still gloomy, fragmented, and crime-ridden downtown.

It struck my mother as strange that Dad would let us go back to the city by ourselves with no adult at the loft to be with us. But that's how he planned it, and the fall semester of school was starting in four days.

I don't think Dad listened to anything my mom said about raising us. He had reluctantly taken custody of us when I was eleven, because mom was "tired" all the time, and as far as the Virginia state court was concerned, those Budweisers kept under her living room chair didn't help. But she got better in Alcoholics Anonymous and always, always, regretted losing her kids. Of course, that made Christmas great for us in the beginning—getting gifts from two separate households—but as we got older, like when we returned from Berlin and high school confusions challenged our loyalties, we weren't able to be with her as much. Thus, the distance took on a more wrenching reality. I decided then to call her every day from wherever I was at the time.

When we finally settled back at the loft after visiting my mom, the fact that Dad and Jane weren't due home for three more days didn't make me celebrate, jump on a train of teenage debauchery, and throw a party. Rather, I did my laundry and cleaned my room and, with a little money from my mom, got some food at the local Grand Union. I was always more comfortable staying home.

The loft had been built by my dad only a few years previously. We had been living on Washington Square in the West Village when Dad got word there was a space opening up in the Fluxhouse cooperative in SoHo. The co-op, on Wooster Street, in the clammy, dirty world below Houston Street, was the first of its kind in SoHo, originally organized by George Maciunas, Yoko Ono, and John Lennon. My dad, dedicated to always being on the edge of time in any world—art, money, real estate—quickly grabbed the broken-down loft and made it a home. Though it wasn't much of one. With looming prints of his artwork and that of Elaine Sturtevant, Andy Warhol, and Roy Lichtenstein on all the walls, home was more of a glass refrigerator of untouchables—too cold to relax in.

Despite that, though, I didn't want to go out. I wanted to stay home and eat Oreos and watch my favorite show, *The Odd Couple*. I had been beaten down by the wasteland of German television, so returning to American fare was a godsend. I must've watched *The Odd Couple* thousands of times. I always had a comfort-zone relationship with the TV and lights. The lights had to be managed in a specific and ordered structure—on and bright during the day, then turned down after 4 p.m. And I only watched old TV shows I had watched before, never new ones. New was too scary.

That first night at home, I climbed into bed for a cozy cloistering. Then, around 9 p.m., Bill Arning called me.

"I'm coming, I'm coming!" (PHOTO BY BILL ARNING)

He was, without question, my best friend at Friends Seminary high school.

4

NUCLEI

FRIENDS SEMINARY IS A QUAKER SCHOOL on the East Side of Manhattan. When I was there in the late 1970s, it was full of rich, white, privileged kids. I went there after spending two years of middle school at St. Luke's in the West Village because my dad felt the public schools in New York City were atrocious. So he kept us in private religious schools, although the religion part was secondary to almost everything else.

Most of the kids at Friends had been there since kindergarten. Although my sister MB and I were not from one of those wealthy families, we were from a well-connected one. Being a critic at *Newsweek* magazine, my dad just charmed the pants off the principal, Joyce McCray, so we were accepted to the school and given scholarships. However, we always felt a little separate. We were acutely aware that we weren't rich and everyone else was. However, none of that mattered when I studied. Although I was eventually pulled away by Bill, music, my rising appetite for the nightclub music scene, and eventually the Student Teachers, I was always deeply connected to my studies.

It's hard for new kids in school, particularly teenagers, to be accepted. They are the insects in the corner trying not to get stepped on. I kept really quiet and just followed the straight line from class to class, then home, as quickly as possible. Oddly, this specific trait was very much who I was, as it was natural and easy for me to slip behind the curtain anywhere and disappear. I think that's why it felt so right to eventually become a drummer—I could hide in the back. But that was not Bill's nature—and he was going to pull me out.

Bill was taller than everyone else. In fact, at six foot four, he towered over the rest of the school, which immediately made him suspect. He also wasn't a jock, which cemented his place in the suspect camp. He stuttered, was chubby, had atrocious acne, and dressed in nondescript slacks and business shirts, which, inside that lily-white school churning out future sorority sisters and Ivy Leaguers, just spotlighted his weirdness. Both the cool kids and the uncool kids flatly ignored him.

Before the revolution. (PHOTO BY BILL ARNING)

But I adored him. He was funny in a brutally original way, and really, really bright. It wasn't as if Bill and I discussed the great struggles we were enduring at that time—we were just kids—but Bill, without fail, was always happy. He was the youngest of three kids and, being the baby, was doted on. Honestly, I think his parents saw him as a remarkable kid and they just supported that. I'm not sure if they knew he was gay. I'm not sure that Bill knew he was gay, either. Nobody ever really talked about it then. But if there was one place where it was a regular and accepted part of life, it was the punk rock scene.

When I first came to Friends the previous year, and being the new kid, I was immediately put in the uncool group as well—discounted, whispered about, and laughed at, so Bill became my protector. I could, literally and figuratively, hide behind him because he was so tall. Better yet, he made me laugh; even better, I could soak up his intellect. In my first semester at Friends, Bill and I studied T. S. Eliot together in a private class with my very first hero, our English teacher, Phil Schwartz.

But even more critically, Bill was a font of knowledge and experience about music in the world and particularly the punk rock scene in downtown New York City. He was a bright star who knew everyone. I want to say the rays emanating from him were just for me, which perhaps they were for a time, but his smarts and artistic sensitivity affected so many of us in the punk scene, it's hard to think it was just me who benefited. But there's no doubt that everything that happened to me in the rock 'n' roll world—the people I met and knew and the work I did— was because Bill was my best buddy at school.

Yet I still thought of myself for a time as "normal," or I tried to be normal despite the ropes dragging me away. Being fourteen and still in my first year of high school, I was in a fragmented state, trying to fit in though I knew in my gut I probably never would. When I finished the fall semester studying Eliot with Mr. Schwartz, I received an A, which was great and, even more important, cemented my passion for literature and academia.

Then, somehow, Bill's other best friend at school, Andrew Owen, decided he liked me. What was peculiar about this was that Andrew was purely and absolutely in the cool kids' camp. In fact, he was the guy all the "cool" girls wanted to date. Andrew was the perfect 1970s *Starsky & Hutch* specimen—puffy long hair, perfectly pressed bell-bottoms and tight pink shirts. He came from one of the richest families in school— his father was the CEO of Seagram—and he was sought after by all the twirly young Farrah Fawcett future sorority girls. But it was me he liked. I was floored.

I tried very hard to look like what I thought he wanted: long hair with the front sides flipped back, cool bell-bottoms, flowy white shirts. I hated dressing like that as much as I liked him. The first time we got to the point of holding hands was at the only dance I ever went to at Friends. It was held in the courtyard and the common room inside. They played songs from the Partridge Family, the Beatles, and the Monkees, gave out fruit sodas and pretzels and urged us to dance, though none of us did. Most kids hung out in the back of the school, with the older students, smoking cigarettes and drinking smuggled-in beer. But not Andrew and me. We just stood in the gym, or in the courtyard, holding hands and talking to Bill, who was there giggling and eating brownies. Then we walked to the front of the school, still holding hands, never letting go, and talked to his friends hanging out there. Or rather, he talked, not me. I kept quiet. Obediently quiet. A church mouse.

When the dance ended and the school lights were turned off, we walked to the corner. It was about 11 p.m. and we each had to depart—me downtown to dark SoHo, and Andrew to the posh Upper

Andrew and me—too scared to look at each other even when we kissed.
(PHOTO BY BILL ARNING)

East Side. A divide in the road, a split in the process, a dismembering of our grasping hands. Bill was with us and he was going to take the bus uptown with Andrew while I ventured to the subway. Bill started walking and Andrew's and my hands separated. He leaned down and gave me a kiss. I felt his lips quivering on my cheek. A petrified rabbit. His whole self was shaking. Me too. I feared I might pass out. Then my hair would be destroyed. I couldn't bear the thought. Then he turned and walked away and I headed to the subway station. It was remarkable how nervous we both were with each other. Was it love? Was that where the uncontrollable fear inside of our stomachs was coming from? It was a strange, unexpected experience for me. And, ironically, I had lost my virginity six months previously, in a heated, unfortunate moment with a guy from Stuyvesant High School. His name was Hootie Hooten, and he was nice, though only a momentary giggle.

The rest of the spring and through the summer, Andrew and I were inseparable. We periodically met on a bench near New York University, in the West Village, and sat and talked. Sometimes we would meet at Central Park and lie on the grass holding each other, sometimes making out but mostly just holding each other. We never had sex. We tried but often quickly stopped. It wasn't that we couldn't. I think it was a belief in him that we shouldn't. And I agreed. I think.

Andrew was with me for a long time in high school, even after I had turned my back on the erudite Friends Seminary world of academics and turned more to the off-color, encrusted world of punk rock. Back in the shadows, though, Andrew was still there, and he saved me more than once.

When I first went to Bill's house to hang out, I was astounded. He lived in a huge apartment near Friends. Like those of all the other kids there, his well-to-do family life was obvious in the plush comfort of his huge home. He had his own bathroom right across the hall from his bedroom. And his bedroom! Wow! There was a huge double bed in the corner, and on the right-hand wall there was an amazing stereo system with two turntables, amps, and speakers; across from there was a floor-to-ceiling bookcase full of records. There must have been more than a thousand albums by artists from the Rolling Stones, Cream, and Led Zeppelin to the Velvet Underground, Patti Smith, the Clash, the

Sex Pistols, the Ramones, and T. Rex. My jaw dropped when I saw it all. He was meticulous about caring for his collection, even though we spent hours and hours listening to them and albums ended up strewn (carefully) around the room.

When Bill called me first thing after I got home from Germany, I was thrilled. He wanted to meet. Except the thing was, I wanted to stay home. It wasn't just that I was tired or recovering from the months of upheaval living in Europe—this was me. I wasn't just a homebody. Deep inside me, pulsing through my bone marrow, I was a bit of a recluse. I think I developed that world-stopping need to stay home as a result of my parents' divorce and the endless disruption—one year living in New York, one year living in Virginia. The constant changing of schools went as far back as to when I was five, when Mom and Dad called it quits.

Except I had been relentlessly forced to defy that part of me, starting with my dad kicking us out of the house all the time. Going out became an act of will on my part. And that's what happened that night when Bill called. He was at Max's Kansas City to see the Mumps and he wanted me to meet him there. Through sheer resolve, I put on my jacket and left the house to see my best friend. To this day, I remember thinking, as I walked down the four flights in my building out the front door to go meet him, that this was definitely not me. But it was Bill.

That was a constant tension, or one of many constant tensions. I was relentlessly aware that I lived against my inner instincts while I was in the punk rock world. And that tension manifested in my love for academia. Don't get me wrong, I hated the structure of school, and it was criminal that I had to be there at 8:15 a.m. every morning, but I loved learning. I loved the academics, studying medieval literature, Old English, and the history of Rome. But at that time, my passion for rock 'n' roll was as deep as my appetite for scholarship, and, somehow, they had to coexist.

. . .

SOHO WAS EMPTY THAT NIGHT. Late-'70s New York was far more sinister than it is today, and it seemed desolate when the sun disappeared. Being a penniless teen, I walked everywhere, and I did so as quickly as possible. Because I was convinced that at night, when I ran home from wherever I was, my shoes would make noise and awaken all the spectral forces lurking behind the trash cans—the thieves, the muggers, the rapists—I walked quietly and speedily. Then I jammed my keys into the front door of our building, shutting and locking it as fast as humanly possible when I got inside.

It was a time that defined what New York came to be famous for being: cold-blooded. It was a time of high crime and little growth, and the powers in charge were too inundated with the city's breakdown to care about cleaning the lingering garbage and homeless off the streets. It was a regular catastrophe as I walked to school or anywhere. So that night, I essentially took my life in my hands by walking down Spring Street to the subway at 9:30 p.m. to go uptown to meet Bill on Seventeenth Street, near Max's. Either out of foolishness or as a means to an end, as time went on, I regularly walked and took the subway late at night in the city, even into the early-morning hours, and I never considered what might happen to me if the stars weren't in my favor.

Bill was waiting out front of Max's, and when I saw him, I raced over and gave him a huge hug. I was overjoyed. Berlin had been such a friendless experience for me, and to be with my best buddy now and going in to see the Mumps—I was dazed with excitement. It felt so right. That was where I belonged.

The funny thing is, this is exactly how it all happened—for many of us. The Sex Pistols, the Clash, Patti Smith, Talking Heads, the Ramones, Blondie—we were rabid fans of these voices and this music. This was a movement of revolution: The energy and the upheaval it caused in the rock 'n' roll world was electrifying because the artists were bringing it directly to us—the fans. This was the end of the world of the big bands of the early 1970s—Led Zeppelin, the Eagles, Pink Floyd, Emerson Lake & Palmer— and of the excesses of major-label stadium rock. It was no longer the goal to go to big arenas to see rock 'n' roll. The important bands evolving at this time were in these small nightclubs. It was happening everywhere but most fervently in New York and London. They were right there for us. It was personal. No longer was it impossible to imagine being in a band and putting out your own records. Because of that, new, innovative groups were springing up all over the world. And I learned all about it from Bill.

Max's Kansas City, like CBGB, became a second home to Bill and me, and the friends we made there eventually became our family.[1] Max's was a two-story nightclub on the East Side of the city, just a few blocks from my high school. There were a bar and a stage on the second floor and a restaurant on the first floor. Max's was a legendary hotbed of creativity and home to the avant-garde art and music scene of the 1960s. Famously, as a hangout for the Andy Warhol crowd, including the Velvet Underground, the club was notorious for sex, drugs, debauchery, and iconic performances by such local luminaries as the New York Dolls, the Harlots of 42nd Street, Teenage Lust, Wayne County, and by Detroit's Iggy and the Stooges. Actually, on one occasion at Max's, Iggy was rushed to the emergency room after he had wounded himself by falling through a table filled with glasses during one of his crowd-surfing sojourns. In the '70s Max's was one of the key venues for the burgeoning music scene.

A half hour later, when the Mumps show was about to start, we ran upstairs to the second floor. The place was packed, but Bill had already saved us some seats in the front. He also paid my entry fee. Being the baby of a wealthy family, he was always covered, and he spread his generosity to all of us.

At first, though, I was a little nervous. Although I had been here for a show before I left for Berlin, something was different. Maybe it was because my dad hadn't returned yet and I was here by myself—in the city by myself—and it was clear that this was the adult world. It was shadowy and moody; people were at the bar drinking and eyeing each other, making out and flirting. The air of naughtiness, sexuality, and hot rock 'n' roll floated throughout the place. I was an alien, a green, calcified underage alien, so I kept close to Bill. He was a regular there and he knew everyone. He was relaxed and fit right in, even though, to me, the club screamed wickedness. That ever-present tension kept biting me, the obscure, mysterious air inside the small nightclub snapping at my heels.

---

1   Philip recalls: "At the time, most of the regulars were 'veteran scenesters' in their twenties and thirties, but there was a countable number of teenage high school kids around, and we all got to know each other from sitting at the front tables at CB's and Max's, or waiting on line for concerts at other venues around the city. We all still know each other."

Upstairs in the front of Max's, three large windows hung over booths and a few tables. The small stage, fifty feet to the back past the bar, was pure black, with no backstage, and thirty seats in front of it. No one cared that Bill and I were teenagers, and when we got to the front door, we were greeted by a beautiful blonde in a skimpy miniskirt and thick red lipstick. She came over and giggled when she saw Bill, then smiled and brushed back my hair with her silver-nailed fingers.

"Jayne, this is Laura," said Bill. I smiled.

"Well, hi, darling, I'm Jayne County," she said, her eyes ringing. "Make sure to come to my show next weekend, ladies!"

She hurried with us to the front. Jayne was the DJ for Max's and she introduced everyone to the punk rock coming out of the U.S. and London and Europe. If it wasn't for her, I don't know what would have happened. And I did go see her show: Jayne County and the Electric Chairs. It was loud and wild and she was an exquisite presence. Turns out, Jayne was the first rock 'n' roll transgender singer. I didn't know that then, and I wonder if anyone did, or even if anyone even cared.

When we sat down, Bill introduced me to Jody Robelo[2] and Lori Reese—our future band's manager and bassist, respectively—and to Michael Alago.[3] They were all kinetic, so dynamic. They handed me a beer and a cigarette right away, even though I didn't smoke and only had a beer once before. They took me right into their enclave—so different from Berlin and that bitter military school there, so very different from my dad.

Bill pushed me to talk to Lori. He had met her at a Sparks show at the Bottom Line. She was a couple years older than me and she smoked and didn't take much crap. She worked at a record store and lived in Brooklyn with her mother. She had dark, curly hair and clever brown eyes like a German shepherd who was sweet but perpetually on guard. We eventually became really close friends, which was odd, at first glance, because we couldn't have been more different. She was the tough, together girl from Brooklyn, and I was the shy, confused blonde trying to escape the Ivy League wannabes at an East Side private high school in Manhattan.

---

2   Jody was copresident of the Dead Boys fan club with Michael Alago.

3   Michael became an A&R executive and signed Metallica to Elektra Records.

We regularly rode the subway at 3 a.m., either to her place after a show or to mine. I remember venturing, one murky late night, to visit a family friend of hers, way out in Queens. We must've been on the subway for two hours, and although I was really nervous because I had never been so far away from home and certainly not that far from Manhattan before, I hid my fears and played the cool, together rock 'n' roller.

Fire and ice. Lori and me. Ecstatic! (PHOTO BY BILL ARNING)

Lori and her friends' world was so different and exotic to me. The foods and smells and rituals were wholly foreign—grandmothers forever at the stove stirring unbelievably tasty sauces and stews, extended family always around the kitchen table, screaming about Ed Koch, then slipping you a five-dollar bill on the side. I had never been around that kind of familial warmth before, and hanging with Lori made me feel welcome and a part of it. It was as if we had both been searching for a best friend and had found that with each other.

Today, that class divide isn't as extreme as it was in 1977, because Brooklyn has now become a golden-blue gentrified tech-hub world, versus in the late '70s, when the borough was the land of established Italian and Hispanic families settling in amid their traditions and time-honored customs. It was in stark contrast to downtown SoHo—grimy and broken and filled solely with white artists and wannabe intellectuals. The gap was wide. Yet despite the disparity of our cultural backgrounds, Lori and I clicked immediately, with that kind of energy where we finished each other's sentences. There are some people you meet in life who become acquaintances, business associates, teammates, or partners in crime. Lori and I were all of those and more. It was a blast, and would ultimately serve us well, because the bass player and drummer form the backbone of a band, and it was essential that we operate as a single-minded unit, especially as our worlds soon collided within themselves. Our connection would manifest itself in a new dimension, as we ended up living together and forming a band with Bill, David, and Philip.

Bill's heartthrob, Lance Loud. (PHOTO BY STEVE LOMBARDI)

As Lori and I talked and sipped Budweisers, Bill kept getting up and walking back to the bar and then back to the table. He seemed to be looking for someone but he didn't say who. Bill was the Mumps' biggest fan and they all knew him. He followed them to every single gig they performed. He knew all their songs by heart and constantly played them on his tape recorder. He was an avid photographer and took pictures of the band at every show. He was obsessed, and his passion for the Mumps was primarily triggered by one person: Lance Loud, the lead singer. And that's who he was looking for that night.

5

THE MUMPS

LANCE LOUD WAS THE FRONT MAN. Kristian Hoffman was the keyboardist and principal songwriter, Rob Duprey was the guitarist, Kevin Kiely was the bass player, and Paul Rutner was the drummer. The Mumps were a high-powered, breathtaking power pop group and a huge favorite in the late-'70s New York rock club world. Essentially, they were Bill's and my reason for being on the punk rock scene in the first place.

The seductive Gang of Five. (PHOTO BY DEBBIE SCHOW)

The Mumps were one of the New York groups that fell into the second echelon of bands, after the Ramones, Talking Heads, Blondie, Television, and Patti Smith. They were popular in New York City and in the East Coast clubs, headlining dates at the Rat in Boston, the Hot Club in Philadelphia, and the 9:30 Club in Washington, DC. They had toured the West Coast a couple of times and were trying to parlay their rising popularity into a record deal with a major label. Their live shows were legendary, but they had yet to capture that magic on tape to get signed. We never missed their shows, and for Bill, more than anything, it was all about Lance.

Lance Loud carried with him some fame because he'd starred in the first Hollywood reality show, titled *An American Family*, in 1973. The show was controversial, as was Lance, who had come out as being gay at a time when being homsexual was offensive and unacceptable to the mainstream populace. He defied that societal condemnation and eventually became a gay rock 'n' roll icon in the New York scene. He was perfect for that role because of his forceful and magnetic personality, which he filtered into the Mumps' exuberant energy. He dominated the stage with his powerful vocals and physical command. He grabbed everyone's attention.

That night when they ran onto the stage the entire audience went wild. They started with their song "Teach Me" and we all got up and danced. I felt happier than I had in such a long time. I knew that this was an easy, if not predictable, way for us teenagers to get out our energy and confused feelings, and it was working. But there was also a spirit in that club, coming from the Mumps as they powered out their music, that actually became way more than that for us. It was centered on the fact that we were accepted in those clubs and by the musicians in those bands—specifically the Mumps—as one of them. Of course, there was the initial setup that we were fans, but underlying this was a recognition of us fifteen- and sixteen-year-olds as potent voices with thoughts and ideas that were as good and interesting as those onstage whom we clapped for and adored. We were treated like MB and I had been by the East Berlin soldiers who didn't care that we were barely teenagers when they searched us on the train: They accepted us—our age wasn't the point. For teenagers lost in a void between childhood and emerging adulthood, that was powerful.

Bill had become closer with Lance and the Mumps while I was in Berlin, and had started to run their fan club. As I joined Bill at their gigs more and more, I started helping him out at the fan club as well. But recording their shows on cassettes, handing out fan club flyers, and helping to publicize the shows via word of mouth wasn't enough. Bill and I decided we needed to do something more and came up with the idea of videotaping them. Although this may seem like a small effort today, in the late '70s, video was cutting-edge and avant-garde. It was an unprecedented phenomenon, like the escalating punk/new wave scene in the clubs. It brought the wall, which normally separated us fans from our rock heroes, completely down. Anyone who wanted to make a video of what they believed was an important event, story, or art piece, or of music they loved, could. And my dad, being one of the leaders of the video avant-garde movement, had equipment and a studio. So I figured Bill and I could use them to film the Mumps.

Bill spreading the word—"The Mumps Are Ideal"—
with Nicole Struensee and Didi Shaw. (COLLECTION OF BILL ARNING)

As we worked on the filming, we became friendlier with all of them, and Bill got even closer to Lance. I don't think they ever became lovers[1] but Bill was devoted to Lance, and, in his own way, Lance was devoted to Bill.

It was exciting and frightening to be in such a familiar, unqualified position with them, especially since we still had geometry exams and term papers to take and write. Yet in many ways, that scholastic reality was fading fast, even though that feather still fluttered at my neck.

One time, all the guys in the Mumps came over to Bill's apartment to view the videos we were making of them. These hadn't been edited yet, so the tapes were rough, but the band wanted to see them anyway. I felt an inner shock wave course through me when they walked in: Rob with his seething, brooding dark mantle of the Detroit cowboy in stark contrast to Kevin's poppy, bright blonde go-go style and Kristian's high-energy, almost kingpin authority. They were followed by Paul, the cute boy of the group, and Lance, who, as he walked down the hall to the room next to Bill's, shook the walls with his overpowering presence.

I literally didn't speak the entire time. Each of them was so good-looking and older and, to a young teenage girl, breathtaking. Bill did all of the talking because he knew Lance and Kristian pretty well, and I just tried not to bumble and mess things up, as I was in charge of the video equipment. But it was so hard to stay focused. Here were these grown men, working in music in a real and professional way, and me and Bill—two teenage fans trying to be more than that to them. Even though I had filmed them for a while and done a lot fan club work, I myself was still just a fan. I had listened to these guys constantly in Berlin—they had saved me. I kept my distance in the clubs when filming them, but then, at Bill's house—there they were, in the same room, watching the video I had made of them playing their songs "Photogenia" and "Muscle Boys." It was surreal. I shook my fear off as much as possible. I tried hard not to blunder and gawk but it was hard—particularly when I found myself standing next to Paul. He didn't notice me. But I really noticed him.

---

1 Bill: "Lance and I definitely never had anything sexual between us: I just tried to turn into him."

Paul, stealing my heart. (PHOTO BY THERESA KEREAKES)

Since my capture by Bowie's Isolar tour at Madison Square Garden, the hold my tape-recorded music had taken of my soul in Berlin, and now, my actual involvement in the New York punk scene—rock 'n' roll had finally imprisoned me. I was a hostage. As I started filming the Mumps more, Bill and I were at the clubs every weekend, and some weeknights, and my life at home started to disintegrate.

6

SENTIENCE

SCHOOL WAS THERE. IT NEVER LEFT. But one thing became clear as I went to the nightclubs more and to Bleecker Bob's to buy records: Money was an issue. Yes, Bill helped out with a lot of expenses related to the taping of the Mumps and getting me into shows, but he couldn't cover everything, and my dad's pockets were sealed. I had to get a job.

One afternoon in the fall of 1977, I went back to my old middle school on Hudson Street—St. Luke's—to check the announcement board in the cafeteria. There was a job posting for a babysitter to pick up a seven-year-old girl after school, take her home, help her with homework, and feed her dinner before her mother got home at 6 p.m. It paid fifty dollars a week and started the following Monday. I called.

That Sunday, I met with Leslie Butler at her house. She was a divorced mom and her daughter, Yancy, was in second grade.[1] Leslie worked as a manager for a Broadway company, planning and setting up shows. They lived in a one-bedroom apartment in a seven-floor walk-up. Leslie slept on the sofa while Yancy slept in the bedroom. There was a small kitchen and an even smaller bathroom. I remember thinking it was odd that they lived in such a small place while Yancy attended an expensive private school.

Every day after I finished at Friends, I raced across town to pick up Yancy. A springy little brunette, she was so much fun, and we had a ball together. When we got back to her house we always watched Adam West's

---

1   Yancy Butler became a well-known actress appearing in the *Kick-Ass* films and starring in the TV series *Witchblade*.

Batman. I don't know if she was allowed to watch that—maybe she was only supposed to watch *Sesame Street*—but she loved it and so did I. I usually made some peanut-butter-and-jelly sandwiches to eat while we watched the Caped Crusader; then we'd do homework, if she had any, until dinner. Leslie usually got home around then.

I became close with Leslie, and we often hung out and talked. She wasn't too tall, had flawless skin and a waterfall of dark hair draping down her back. She was funny and warm and loved to gab. Although they seemed happy, it struck me that theirs were not the easiest of lives. Later, I learned that Yancy's father was Joe Butler, the drummer of Lovin' Spoonful. I guess I thought that the life of a rock star's daughter would be better than it seemed in that small, fusty apartment. But I was learning that life was rarely what I thought it should be.

Home was a traffic stop. I was there—sleeping, going to school, doing homework. But I was very far away. My father was barely aware of my absence, as his work at *Newsweek* kept him chained to his typewriter. Although he had moments where he suddenly realized that MB and I were in residence, he merely saw us through the lens of himself. It seemed that the rest of the city functioned much the same way as my dad. Despite the ghost of control and structure dancing through our teenage lives, we were on our own. We were never carded at clubs or stopped when adults saw us smoking and drinking. We were one of them, and at CBGB and Max's, that was even more clear-cut.

CBGB (or CBGB OMFUG, as it was officially called) was the star horse of the punk rock scene at that time, stationed on the Lower East Side of Manhattan. Everyone jumped on its back and Hilly Kristal, the famed owner, was more than happy to take on newcomers. Besides booking more established acts, he provided space for newer, younger, punkier bands. Much as the Roxy and 100 Club in London provided a haven for the developing punk rock scene there, with the Sex Pistols, the Damned, and the Clash, CB's played host to a similar, earlier revolution in New York City.

At that time, CBGB was a dark, wood-paneled club that looked like it should have been for sports geeks, with mugs of beer at the bar and the latest Yankees stats posted on the walls. It was long, with booths on the left side and a shadowy bar down the right wall. At the end of the bar was a dancing space and a bunch of chairs and tables in front of a corner stage overseen by two giant photos of Victorian spinsters. Upstairs, there was a shelter for homeless men. The neighborhood, comprised of crumbling buildings built in the 1800s and ignored by their current owners, was falling apart, like most of the downtown area. Garbage and ruined lives were everywhere. Cracked delirium spilled out wherever you walked. What once had been a vibrant home for immigrants and early New Yorkers was a wasteland.

So hanging outside of CB's was a risk, but for us penniless teens and lost souls, it was a necessity. CB's—and Max's, a mile uptown—were portals of unrest and searching, where screaming and introspective new music was being created. They were also places where alliances, romances, and bands were constantly forming.

The door of CB's was run by a big buffalo of a man named Merv Ferguson, who managed the place. He pretended to be tough, and he bounced a few drunks every now and then but, more than anything, he was a teddy bear. Whenever I went there he gave me a big hug and smile and welcomed me in. But it wasn't just me he was so sweet to—it was everybody. I often had this fantasy of seeing Merv and Hilly—those two old guys—at a poker game late one night slamming back shots of whiskey and joking about starting a club on the Lower East Side of the city because the rent was cheap and they could sell overpriced drinks. And that's what happened. Except it became far more than that.

Merv's usual cohost at the door was Roberta Bayley. Roberta was a vibrant young woman from California, who found herself in New York, working at CB's. She was witty and bright, with shining auburn hair. As she helped run the door at CB's, she developed her burgeoning photography skills and rose in the ranks as a celebrated rock photographer known most widely for taking the famous photo of the Ramones that graced the cover of their first album. Every guy onstage at CB's thirsted for her. She was a star on the scene in her own right. It was a notable and landmark personal accomplishment when Roberta deigned to give you "the nod" to enter the club without having to pay. It verified your status as either being in a band she liked or a CB's regular. It was thrilling, welcoming, and affirmed that you belonged.

While at CB's and Max's on the weekends, Lori and I made friends with a band called the Erasers. They were a mostly all-girl band with one guy—the guitar player, Richie Lure—and they had grown out of the downtown art scene. Susan Springfield was the lead singer and she was high-energy, thoughtful, and smart. We ended up working as their roadies—helping them move their equipment around and setting up their shows. They lived in a loft in downtown Manhattan two blocks from CBGB. Like those of many young artists and musicians settling into the downtown neighborhoods, their loft was huge, with bright brick walls and gigantic front windows. Susan and the bass player, Jody Beach[2], and the drummer, Jane Fire, lived and rehearsed there because the main room, like all of the emerging lofts downtown—was big enough for a live band and the raucous sound it made.

When we started working for the Erasers, I began to feel like a real adult, as if I were their age: twenty-three, twenty-four, a grown-up rock 'n' roller who was now a roadie for a band. Lori and I were backstage at all their shows, lifting amps and drums and speakers and setting up the stage so the band could perform and make great music. It was an amazing feeling of responsibility—to make sure the show went on without a problem. Lori and I were important. I wasn't a minor eleventh grader going to high school every day.

Except I was.

One night in December 1977, I was at home in SoHo getting ready to go to an Erasers show at CB's. Lori was with me, and before we left to get the equipment, my stepmother, Jane, put on a Christmas special where David Bowie was singing "Silent Night" with Bing Crosby. My usual frantic self, excited and blazed to get going, was thrown into a full stop.

Bowie—that Garden show roared back to me. There he was, singing with Bing Crosby. He was so commanding, imperial—otherworldly. Their collaboration was considered historic at the time, because it was one of the first times a rock 'n' roller had sung with a traditionally known "popular" singer. It made us all rethink rock 'n' roll as more than a response to angry adolescent frustrations. Since then, the practice has become far more commonplace, with the likes of Frank Sinatra, Tony Bennett, Tom Jones, and even Barbra Streisand releasing entire albums of duets with such unlikely partners as the Art of Noise, Cyndi Lauper, U2, and Lady Gaga.

---

2   Jody ended up marrying Chris Spedding, and they are still actively working in music while living in England.

As I stood there with Lori watching Bowie sing, I gulped clouds of air down my throat, mesmerized by him. I had followed him feverishly since the Garden show and his *Aladdin Sane* album, which then threw me into *The Rise and Fall of Ziggy Stardust and the Spiders from Mars*. He captured me as he had captured so many others. My obsession was certainly nothing unique. I was just another small voice nowhere near his orbit. He seized me, body and soul, as water saves a dying person. He gave me purpose in an unspoken way that was not dependent on trying to know him or sleep with him or be physically close to him. It was similar to when I read the work of a great poet, novelist, or philosopher—it changed me. He altered the way I perceived meaning.

7

FROM THE EYE-CATCHER TO THE CAUGHT

THEN MY WORLD BECAME EXTREMELY COMPLICATED.

Around a year earlier, in 1976, at a John Cale concert, Bill met David Scharff and Philip Shelley. Then, a little while later, they met Lori at a Patti Smith poetry reading at the Bottom Line. This was not atypical of the opportunities available nearly every week, to see incredible artists at either the peak of their powers or in the early stages of their brilliant careers.

Although I wouldn't meet them for another year, David and Philip fell into two exposed and hungry spaces within our group, transforming all of us.

That's where the spirit came from in the downtown punk scene. It was not just hyper teenage energy but the desire of many who wanted— needed—a voice. And the punk scene provided that megaphone for all of us. It fired up Television, the Heartbreakers, Talking Heads, the B-52s, Patti Smith, Blondie. But an important difference was that the energy we brought to those bands as fans, spectators, followers, was part of a dialectic. The vitality of the musicians and their music bounced back to them on the stage. Stadium acts played their music at us, not with us: a very new dynamic evolved between us and the bands in these tiny clubs. We were in it together. And although most of those musicians onstage were quite a bit older than my friends and me, and though our experience of the downtown scene wasn't precisely as theirs was, in many ways our desires, frustrations, anger, and aspirations were exactly the same.

The roadie work Lori and I were doing for the Erasers piqued our excitement about the world behind the stage. Being a part of the mounting of a rock 'n' roll show fired our imaginations and ideas. And hanging with a crowd of fervent rock 'n' rollers like the Erasers, the Mumps, the Blessed, and the Cramps showed Bill, Lori, and me that we could do it too—we could and should start a band.

By mid-fall of '77, we all had a meeting at Bill's house. It was a vivid October Saturday, swirling with a smooth, bright sky. Lori, Michael Alago, and I were hanging out, listening to *The Slider* by T. Rex. Lori and Michael sat near an open window while she smoked and the crisp air blew in. The front doorbell rang, and Bill ran down the hall. A minute later, David and Philip came in. Lori and Michael knew them, but this was my first meeting. David was tall, slim, and dark with tight leather jeans and a cocky coolness. Philip was the exact opposite. Shorter, with dirty-blonde hair blowing across his head, he had a well-worn scowl, which loosened with his manic excitement as he ducked into the room.

My initial impression of David and Philip was, at best, knotty. I guess what I saw at first were two rich white boys from the tiny suburbs of Larchmont, eager to live the fantasy of the city's meaty world—the land of shadowy, dirty rock 'n' roll.

But Bill and Lori and I—we knew that meat. It lived around us every day—not just in the clubs, but on the sidewalks of the blue, crisis-ridden city. We kicked garbage on the street on our way to school. We were embryonic garbage spawned from the city wreckage going to play punk in the clubs—not foreigners from beyond the city limits coming in to have the "big-city experience."

I couldn't have been more wrong.

Philip was in a punk rock group in Larchmont called Jo Ckitch, and they had just released a single, which David had engineered in a small recording studio at his house. They were big Patti Smith followers and Jonathan Richman lovers. In fact, Bill had taken both of them out for a drink after they'd all attended a Jonathan Richman concert at NYU, and had asked if they wanted to join a band. Even more significantly, Bill had a crush on David. Bill's infatuations always led to the creation of any given concept quivering in the air above all of us.

For example, our plan during that first meeting at Bill's was to do more than discuss becoming a band; rather, we meant to set it up right then and there. It had been considered that Lori would be the singer but Bill convinced her that David would make a really good front man. Philip was already a guitar player, so it was decided Lori and I would be the rhythm section—the girl rhythm section. I would take the drums and Lori would take the bass. We had been inspired by the Erasers' all-girl dynamic and we thought it was a great idea to continue building that muscle.[1]

Then, because Bill had a crush on a student teacher in our geometry class at school, we decided to name our band the Student Teachers. There we were. Concept created. Bill's wandering heart was the soil of a lot of our growth.

We also posed for a photo shoot at that first meeting. The photos, taken by Michael, were for our first poster, shouting "Student Teachers! Lesson One: Coming Soon!" and were pasted everywhere across downtown New York. That first photo shoot, that first poster were in many ways a fantasy, a pretense. That was not unusual—it was a manifestation of the yearning, the rumbling throughout every rock club in the city. It also may have been fuel for our teenage angst or turmoil at that time, but it didn't feel that way. It felt like we could do something real.

It didn't matter that neither Lori nor I knew how to play our instruments yet. Granted, there were many remarkable musicians and songwriters on the scene, including John Cale, Television's Richard Lloyd and Tom Verlaine, Bob Quine and Ivan Julian from Richard Hell's Voidoids. But even Richard Hell and Tina Weymouth had been new to the bass when the Voidoids and the Talking Heads launched.

It was the art creating the artist, the song creating the writer, the music creating the musician. And it grew out of the unique momentum in the punk scene.

When we met David and Philip, we were all in a moment in time, connecting with one another, moving to places and experiences we'd never imagined. It pushed us physically from the seat in the front row below

---

1   Lori's memory is that we had decided already to be a rhythm section before we got together to work with the Erasers.

the stage, up onto the stage, looking out at ourselves—moving from the perceiver to the perceived, from the lover to the loved. It changed us. The change was good and the change was bad—and it was irreversible.

Our first rehearsals were at my drum teacher's loft.[2] It was on the West Side in the Thirties. I had been referred to him by someone at CBGB. His name was Doug. He never took a bath and had greasy black hair and moon-pale skin, with dark brown moles everywhere.

Even though the sharpening downtown art scene where I lived in SoHo was bursting with lofts and working homes built out of old warehouses, the West Thirties was also stumbling into the same sort of renaissance. Those West Thirties buildings had originally served the evolving fashion industry in Manhattan—vacated button buildings and sewing factories were now occupied by dozens of musicians and artists, and the bonus was that, thanks to their cement walls, these spacious old buildings were soundproof. Many rehearsal studios and, ultimately, recording studios popped up everywhere.

Doug's loft was one of the first. He was a really nice guy, and he was patient and encouraging. I went there one or two afternoons every week, after school, while Lori studied bass with his friend.[3]

The first time I sat behind the drum set I felt completely disoriented. It was exciting but really scary. I was the new kid in the class called up to the blackboard by the teacher, then peeing in her pants in front of everyone.

My first lesson with Doug ended up awkward at best. He sat behind the drum set and showed me the basic drumbeat—in 4/4 time—that he wanted me to repeat. Immediately, I felt the oily beads of this snake-oil scheme of mine begin to slide down my face, revealing me for the phony I actually was, showing where I truly belonged—back in Mr. Schwartz's Middle English class.

But Doug evidently didn't notice that I was a sham and handed me his sticks. He started to explain the different stick weights and why I should use 5A—mostly because I was a beginner. I sighed heavily. Then he helped me put my right foot on the bass drum pedal and my left on the hi-hat pedal. As he started talking through a 4/4 rhythm and snapping

---

2   David says, "That loft was where we formed ourselves."

3   Of note: Lori only took two bass lessons. She used her natural sense of music to forge ahead on her own.

Aaagh! I'm playing the drums! (PHOTO BY ROBERT LEVITT)

it with his fingers, he directed me to hit the bass drum in 4/4 time—snap, snap, snap—then he had me hit the hi-hat while continuing to pound the bass drum. Okay, it felt weird but not that difficult, at least at first. But then he instructed me to start hitting the snare drum with the stick in my left hand at the same time: I had to coordinate pounding the bass drum with hitting the snare drum, alternately. I thought I might faint. What was he doing to me? I just wanted to keep the beat.[4]

That was the idea. It was always the idea. David would make a great singer and how interesting, how unprecedented, it would be to have a female rhythm section. Bands, theater groups, performance groups, any art collective, stems from an idea, a concept, a shared perspective, as we did then. But I remember thinking—in a very young, uneducated way—

---

4   Philip says: "I remember Peter Crowley [the booking agent at Max's] lecturing us in the Max's dressing room once, saying that you (Laura) were great and that the only difference between you and Chris Frantz was a few fills that you would eventually learn. It's too bad you never got to play drums for a long time, because you did have a really good basic beat—the kind you can't teach."

that me becoming a drummer was just a terrific scheme for us. It would be so different and new to the scene. Both Bill and Philip knew their instruments, had learned them as they grew up. But I'd never thought of becoming a drummer before—ever.

Yet here I was.

I followed Doug's rhythmic pace as he wandered in front of me, holding the rhythm with his snapping. I started hitting the snare on every other beat, pounding the bass, bringing the right stick over the hi-hat—it felt insane to my body. My brain was tangled up—I was completely losing any sense of myself as I was forced into this alien structure. I learned later that this is referred to as "independence" of the limbs, which a drummer has to incorporate. And it freaked me out.

Suddenly, the stick in my left hand slipped out and I dropped my other stick. I kept pounding the bass drum as I tried leaning over to get them off the floor while Doug kept snapping out the time, ignoring my mess-up, expecting me to get it together and regain control. And I did. But it was hard. Chaucer in my English lit class was easier.

Doug ended up letting our band rehearse in his space, and he gave me some basic rhythm ideas for certain songs as we put them together. He had his own band, but I only went to see them once at a party and I didn't like them at all. Or rather, I felt terrifically intimidated by them. His band was a hard-hitting classic rock group like AC/DC, and when I saw him play, not only was the music annoying to me, but his drum playing seemed far beyond anything I could ever possibly do.

We kept this same beat structure going for the next six weeks with Doug additionally showing me how to hit the ride cymbal in regular time as I had on the hi-hat and how to use the hi-hat pedal to create a sustained sound. Slowly, slowly, I started to get it.

Yet during this frantic time, we still continued filming the Mumps. One night at Max's, when they were playing a gig with the Cramps, we set up the video camera and the video tape recorder on a table about thirty feet back from the stage. I hovered behind the eyepiece and carefully watched them through the lens. As usual, Lance's energy overtook the stage, and his sweat drenched the first three rows of the audience. I moved the camera around as he sang and bounced, then shifted to focus on Rob banging on his guitar, to Kristian singing and playing the keyboard, to Kevin carefully playing the bass rhythm, and to Paul on the drums. And then back to Lance, but suddenly, I swerved the camera back to Paul, then away, then back to Paul again. What was I doing?

Later, as the Mumps were packing up their instruments and Bill and Lori and I organized the video equipment, we went to tell Lance and Kristian about when the editing would be finished. But then Paul abruptly came over and asked if he could see the tape before the editing was finished. Bill turned to me for an answer. I looked at Paul and gulped.

"Sure," I said, hesitating a little; then I quickly went back to packing up the equipment.

As the band lugged their gear out the front door, Bill and I followed. Bill invited the guys to the restaurant beneath Max's club for a late-night bite while I looked for a cab in which to take the video equipment home. But I was suddenly stopped by Paul.

"Come with us for something to eat," he offered. "We'll lock your equipment in my car, okay?"

Despite my unexpected panic, I agreed, and went to eat with the band and Bill. Throughout the entire meal though I barely spoke a word because I couldn't believe Paul had invited me to go with them. I was frozen with both exhilaration and confusion.

At around 1 a.m., we finished eating and Paul and I went to his car so I could get my equipment from his trunk. But I didn't want to get my equipment. As we approached his car, I felt his hand take mine. I smiled and tried hard to not show my excitement.

We ended up going out to Paul's house in Long Island, and because I went with him, and because I was supposed to have gone home, and because I didn't ask my dad's permission to stay out overnight, Paul's phone bellowed a foreboding ring at ten the next morning. It was my dad, screaming the end of the world at me.

Paul quickly drove me back to my home in SoHo. He was worried about what might happen, as my dad had blown the speakers off the phone. I tried to calm him down, telling him I was sure everything would be fine.

Except it wasn't.

When I got upstairs, I walked very carefully into the loft. I peeked around the front closet into the main room. Everything was quiet. I swiftly put the video equipment back in my dad's workroom and went into my bedroom. Five minutes later my door flew open and Dad stood there, shouting out from beneath his blood-red eyes that I better get myself into the living room and explain who the hell I thought I was that I could stay out all night without asking his permission.

Good question.

And I had far from a good answer.

I didn't know who I was. I was living a dual existence and it was getting very hard. But I had some distant, obscure idea of how I wanted to live, and it wasn't according to my dad's plan. I knew without question that I intended to continue playing drums in the Student Teachers, keep filming and helping with the Mumps fan club, and going to CBGB and Max's regularly. Even though I knew in my heart that I would continue going to school, my plans didn't sit well with him. After I weathered my dad's rage, he told me to get out. He'd had enough. He gave me ten minutes and I was to be gone.

I left with as much as I could carry and so did MB, thanks to Dad. She ended up staying at her friend's house in Gramercy Park and I crashed at Bill's. Thinking about it now, I can understand my dad's exhaustion with us obstinate kids, but the response from him was poorly thought-out, because although my stay-over at Bill's was short, my absence from my home in SoHo, to which I returned only a few times, lasted three years, and my relationship with my dad never fully recovered.

8

EXORCISED

DURING MY HOMELESS PHASE, I kept up my drum lessons as well as school. I had a Middle English exam the week after I was kicked out of the house, and I absolutely couldn't miss it or the gods of academia would boil me alive. I was sure of it.

Meanwhile, the band finally started playing together. Our first rehearsals were at Doug's loft. It was a truly strange feeling to me. It was one thing to be playing an instrument alone learning a specific chord—or beat, in my case—with a teacher, then practicing and playing it back to the teacher. But with everyone else coming in, I had to learn how to coordinate the whole thing with the rest of the instruments in the band.

At the first rehearsal, I was behind Doug's drum set and Lori, using her old teacher's bass, was to the left with Bill on his keyboard in front of her. Philip was to the right of me, and David, totally seething with frontman vibe, was reeling with anticipation in the center. My hands felt tingly and shook, and I could see the rest of the guys were anxious too. Could we do this? David was dancing with the mic in his hand and we hadn't even started the song yet.

In many ways, David was the prime force behind our teetering, incubating group. Although there was no hierarchy within us, somehow it always felt as if David not only adored being the front man, he needed it. I don't know what fed that need, but in so many ways it strengthened us and invigorated us. Classically handsome, with intense eyes and a playful sexiness, he approached the stage with a vigorous childlike abandon. And it all started percolating at that earliest rehearsal.

The first songs we practiced were "Captain Kelly," which was about a smoke detector, and "Real World Fun," about watching too much TV.[1]

I saw James at fifteen get devirginized
Kirk and Spock were on at six and four
Twilight Zone used to be on twice a day
But they don't schedule TV like that anymore

The music sounded nearly together even though I wasn't really listening to the other guys. I was just trying to keep a steady beat: 4/4. That was it, and I threw myself into it, making myself a part of it—basically connected only to that. Except that may have been the problem. And it likely didn't help that I had my text of *Beowulf* splayed open just below the snare drum so I could quickly read the underlined sections for the test coming up.

It's not that we sounded bad, but we sounded strained. We were trying too hard—awkwardly, in a virginal way. At one point, Doug, who had been watching and listening, stopped us and talked to everyone about making our playing a little more coordinated and a little more relaxed. Not improvisational, but more as a single unit. An easy, single unit.

Then he walked over to me and told me to listen to the others, really listen, that they were depending on me. I was the backbone, he said and rubbed my super-tense neck. Despite his moles and his AC/DC-self, he was a good guy.

I followed his direction and tried listening to the rest of the instruments more and to get a sense of the wholeness of the song. It was so strange at first to play to the other instruments, rather than to Doug snapping the beat out in front of me. When I realized that I, the drummer, was the one who had to carry the song in a very primal way, I was unnerved. Adjusting to the fact that the drummer affected the entire process, was the one who set the scene for everything else being created, was daunting. In fact, I began to get even more scared about it and decided to stay very fundamental. I didn't want to throw anyone or any song progression off so I didn't veer too far from that basic, metronomic beat: 4/4, 4/4, 4/4.

---

1   Philip: "It's basically [about] seeing the world as an alien landscape or a bad acid trip."

Most of the songs that we played were brought in by Philip and Bill, who were largely the most musical members of the group. But at that time, we decided that all the songs that would come out of our rehearsals and ultimately onto stage, would actually be by the entire band: the Student Teachers. We basically believed that a song really wasn't fully realized, wasn't complete, wasn't truly a song, until we'd all worked it through in rehearsal. I used what I thought would be the best drumbeat,

First rehearsal at Doug's loft. (PHOTO BY ROBERT LEVITT)

Lori added what she felt was the best bass part, and David worked with the lyrics and the melody. This approach changed when we got older and our recordings began bringing in royalties—but at that time, when we were young and first forming, lost in our own lives together, this approach further secured us to one another. We needed that.

As the band started so soon after I'd learned to play the drums, I didn't attempt—nor was I able—to do anything inspired or too improvisational, or even anything athletic like running my sticks over the entire drum kit with flourish and abandon. Maybe I felt that was too "male." And there I was, a female in a traditionally male role. And this was a small new wave pop band, not a searing heavy metal outfit with a drummer who'd built ten snares, two bass drums, three toms, and dozens of cymbals around himself: This was a basic drum set and I was just trying to keep up.

Jody, our true leader. (PHOTO BY STEVE LOMBARDI)

As we continued rehearsing at Doug's loft, Bill arranged for us to do a show at our high school, Friends. Doug encouraged me to continue my drum lessons for a while first. And he was right—I needed more instruction, more practice. But the problem was that I didn't have any more time. Our first gig was in two weeks.

We moved our rehearsals to a space a few blocks south as we prepared for the Friends show. These rehearsals were set up for us by Jody, our official manager at that point. This small, adorable woman turned out to be a powerhouse. She worked as a travel agent during the day but when the workday ended, she organized us, planned our gig schedules, handled booking agents, talked each of us through our teenage loves and losses, and basically rescued us. Even though she was only a year or two older, she was so far beyond all of us.

The new rehearsal studio was more professional than Doug's loft and cost more. Luckily, Bill supported our costs from time to time—paying for rehearsals, transportation, poster ads—but not always. Money was always the horn of the dilemma for us.[2]

We were visited at this studio by Glenn Tilbrook and Harri Kakoulli from the band Squeeze, who were friends with Lori and Antone, and they liked our sound after listening to us.[3] They even played around on our equipment with their song "Take Me I'm Yours." They were in the city from England for their first U.S. shows. Connecting with more established groups gave us a strong sense of viability. The Squeeze guys even wanted to record us and though that never happened, it meant a lot that they hoped to do it. It helped us start believing in ourselves.

One of the best things to come out of those early rehearsals was that we always got together afterward at the McDonald's around the corner. After ordering Big Macs, fries, and chocolate milk shakes, we crowded around a table to plan future gigs, talk about the songs we were working

---

2 David: "We were so ragtag. Everyone but Bill was borrowing. We ended up using money from gigs to buy instruments—which means we had many gigs with borrowed instruments."

3 Lori recalls that she and Antone picked up Glenn and Harri outside of the Chelsea Hotel when they went to pick up a friend. Lori and Antone told them we were going to our little band rehearsal and they asked if they could come. However, Antone says we didn't meet them until the following year after Squeeze opened for Blondie at the club My Father's Place. And Jody says: "Antone and I met Glenn Tilbrook from Squeeze on his first day in New York City and took him to—where else—Bill's apartment. It's actually a pretty funny story of that time—that I am sure Antone can tell better than I can. Memories are fickle."

on and, more than anything, just be together. It was an important connection, because at that time, for many reasons, it was all each of us had. Being a couple years older, Jody and Lori worked, while the rest of us were still in high school—so demands had to be met by all of us. But within the courtyard of the nine-to-five grind and the term papers and the schedules, we belonged to each other. First. Our band took us away from the repetitiveness and programming of life and threw us into something bigger, reverberating with color and highly unpredictable, thanks to the emerging punk rock scene at that time. We were finally able to add our voice, another small dimension to it all.

Amid this second round of rehearsals and before our first gig, David pulled me aside one evening at McDonald's and told me Philip liked me. I was dumbfounded. I'd never had a hint that he did, and I'd known I liked him from the day of the first meeting of the band. But I was still sort of with Andrew. Though "sort of" wasn't written in stone, because Philip and I ended up dating for the next year. This relationship, though very

Philip liked me. (PHOTO BY STEVE LOMBARDI)

Honeymooning at McDonald's. (PHOTO BY ROBERT LEVITT)

helpful in bonding our band even tighter together, also became one of the catalysts of change in my life.

Philip was a unique, highly sensitive, and remarkably bright guy. He adored his Stratocaster and quickly became expert on it. He wrote incredibly good songs without much thought, and, between his alcoholic binges and his manic love of the punk rock world, he was seethingly cool and, to my fifteen-year-old heart, an unexpected dream. We spent as much time as we could together. Since he and David both lived about forty minutes outside of New York and went to Mamaroneck High School, I took the train and visited him as often as possible. It was another very different world and one I had to incorporate into my sense of order—the lands beyond New York City.

Unfortunately, when you are raised in the city, very early on you form an opinion that there is no place in the world like it and, even worse, that it is the only place worth existing in. That instinctive belief gives a sense of euphoria about living there but ruins your chance to find joy somewhere else. It closes your heart. That was my problem, and my forays into suburbia became disruptive to my psyche. Cars; dark, empty streets;

open lawns of grass and trees; houses unconnected to other houses; unobstructed views; no sounds of a world outside your window—it was disturbingly different for me. But that's where Philip lived.

9

DALTON V. TRINITY

OUR FIRST GIG AT FRIENDS IN MARCH '78 took place in the gym. It was held during break period after lunch. The gym, which had recently been constructed in the basement of the school, replacing the small asphalt courtyard outside for phys ed, was a huge regulation educational sports hall. The staff and the students were really pumped to see Friends enter the school sports world with greater seriousness and commitment than before.

When we arrived with our equipment in tow, the place was empty and we set up in the corner of the basketball court. The lights were bright and the basketball hoops had been turned upward. There was very little sense that we were a rock 'n' roll band planning to eventually play in the nightclub world of professional musicians and artists. It felt more like we were a teeny band who play at their best friends' parties.

After we set up, my eyes sped around the gym and I caught the disapproving look of the basketball coach watching us from the far corner. I hung my head as I felt his gaze, purple hot with judgment. I'd known he would be displeased over seeing me here like this, because I was the captain of the girls' basketball team—*his* girls' basketball team—and his basketball players didn't appear in rock bands. I knew he would push my ass into the ground during practice that afternoon. And he did.

I dashed to the locker room after shaking off my coach's disdain and paced back and forth. I must have changed into basketball shorts thousands of times here to play a game against Dalton or Trinity or

Marymount or any of the other teams in the private-school basketball league. But now was different.

Lori was lying on a bench, very cool about it all.[1] She was one of my best friends at that point. She just kept tracing riffs on her bass, sneaking a smoke, and reminding me to chill. But my nerves just kept trembling.

The decision to play at my school was purely a stepping-stone for the band, a test for us and where we wanted to go. I knew that, but it marked the beginning of the breakdown of my structures. At this show, my dual existences of school and the punk rock world irrevocably smashed into one another. I was still close to Andrew even though I was dating Philip, and I still studied madly for Mr. Schwartz's medieval literature class. And, of course, there was the basketball team I played on in that very gym. It was all colliding, and they all couldn't survive. Something had to go.

About fifty kids ended up coming to the show, and we got a terrific reaction. It made us feel like we were on the right wave, that we were doing something that was actually really good. After the show, I helped the group pack up as quickly as I could. David, Philip, and Lori took care of lugging the equipment[2] to Bill's house, but I couldn't go with them. I had to get to my geometry class.

One week after the Friends show, we had our first gig on the club scene at Max's Kansas City.[3] We were the opening act for the Blessed, another young band hailed as just a teenage punk party but who were so much more.

This was a world away from Friends and a world away from life as a teenage wannabe. This was the big time for us, and we were filled with as much fear as exhilaration about it. We had a pretty loyal following of fans now, including Antone DeSantis, who became our roadie. Antone took charge of our equipment and, with Jody, our world. He was tall and dark with toasty skin, bright chestnut eyes, and an unending smile. He was

---

1 Lori actually cut her finger on the pickup at this gig and bled onto her bass, her white bass, which she had borrowed from her teacher.

2 I borrowed Doug's drums for this gig and the next few. David remembers having to reassemble the entire kit back in Doug's loft in the exact same place as it was—as if it had never been touched.

3 David: "I remember us being a little panicked that we had so little material to fill a set with and that we would have to be ready to play in front of a 'real' audience."

Faithful roadie Antone. (PHOTO BY STEVE LOMBARDI)

also a rock scene expert. He knew as much as Bill. There were also Bill's countless friends and David and Philip's Larchmont buddies—Ellen, Sandra, Eloise, Robert, Billy, Matthew, and Jim, and so many more—they were all there. It was like parents coming to support you when you graduate college. And that was us—graduating into the adult world of rock 'n' roll.

Before we were called to the stage, I remember being in the dressing room, which was upstairs at Max's, and gearing up to go on. The rooms were down the hall from the office of the club's booking agent, Peter Crowley. They were small and covered with graffiti—everyone who had played at Max's left their mark on the wall. I was more than nervous and running through beat sequences in my head—the chords changes in the songs, the set list. I was frantic. I grabbed one of Lori's cigarettes, put it in my mouth, and impatiently tapped my foot. If we were going to go through with this operation, I thought to myself, just stick the needle in already.

Lori sat in the corner puffing and Bill was pacing. David put on his stage makeup. Then I looked over at Philip. He was turned away from me, from all of us, facing the back corner of the room. The walls were covered in cracked, inflamed paint that I expected someone had thrown at it one night in an alcoholic stupor. Then I noticed Philip pull a full bottle of NyQuil out of his pocket and down the whole thing in one gulp. I jumped up to see if he was all right but stopped myself when he turned around and grabbed a smoke from Lori. He smiled, sat down, and gave me a kiss. A cherry-flavored menthol kiss. He giggled and grabbed his Strat. He was fine. And he didn't seem to have a cold.

First real gig: I think I can do this. (PHOTO BY ROBERT LEVITT)

We were never denied alcohol at Max's or any of the clubs—as performers or even customers. We were never carded or questioned about our age, so we all drank freely, and often. But it was one thing to have a beer after rolling off the stage to cheers and applause after a show, and another to drink a full bottle of NyQuil before going on. Philip knew that. I was worried.

First real gig: Philip. (PHOTO BY ROBERT LEVITT)

Finally, we were called to start our set. There was no backstage entrance onto the Max's stage, so bands ran through the audience to get up there.

The stage was small and narrow and black. And it was electric. When I sat down behind the drums, I looked out into the audience and almost fell forward onto my bass drum. This was it. I couldn't see anyone out there because of the stage lights, and my palms trembled a little as I held my sticks. I rubbed my legs and watched Philip and Lori anxiously plug into

First real gig: Lori, David, and Bill. (PHOTO BY ROBERT LEVITT)

their amps and quickly tune up. Bill was testing his keyboard and David was jumping up and down, falling from side to side with the mic stand. I peered down at my bass drum. Oh no—I quickly flashed a panicked look at Jody. Knowing my thought, she ran over and quickly taped the set list onto my bass drum. "The Quake"—that was the first song. Okay, okay . . . I was ready. I looked around. Lori was ready; Philip was bouncing; David and Bill looked at each other, then at me. I counted off—one, two, three—the stage lights came on, and David started singing:

> Some people twitch to Christianity
> In Michigan, it's polygamy
> Then there's folks who do it Mormon
> Finding Baptist close to boredom
>
> A shiver up my spine
> My stomach starts to shake
> My ears begin to melt
> And my hips begin to ache
>
> Hey baby! I'm doin' the Quake![4]

---

4   Music and lyrics by Bill Arning, 1979.

Our friends in the front rows jumped and danced and sang. They were loud and bouncing—we all laughed and smiled so hard I thought each one of us would burst into splashing, fleshy pieces of wannabe punks. It was unbelievable.

We played for twenty-five minutes; then we ran off the stage and up the stairs hearing our friends scream wildly behind us. It felt unreal. We fell into the backstage, throwing towels over our wet heads. It wasn't my high school gym; it wasn't a party in the suburbs. It was a nightclub in New York City and we'd done it. We were the real thing.

After all our friends came upstairs to congratulate us, and we cleaned up, we headed back to the stage to help Antone pack. Because we were the opening act, we had to get offstage quickly. Antone took our instruments to his van and the rest of us went to a booth in the front of the club to have White Russians and watch the Blessed, who were onstage next. On my way to the booth I was stopped by a guy I didn't know. His cheeks were a little blown out and he stammered, but he told me he thought I was great, then asked me for my autograph. My what? I was speechless. Why, at this time? This was just our first show—and I wasn't really a drummer, I thought to myself. But I signed it and smiled. He asked when we were playing next but I didn't know. I told him to watch the ads in the back of the *Village Voice*. He smiled at me, then I raced to the booth and grabbed one of the White Russians, shaking my head. I couldn't believe that night.

After the Blessed played and Philip and David exhausted themselves slam-dancing, I joined them and a bunch of the Larchmont allies in a drive back home. It was near 3 a.m. and as tired as we all were, the alcohol had burned off and we were on a buzz high from the show.

We didn't think of ourselves as rock stars, but within our broad, edgy teenage selves we believed we had something, and, even more important, we were now part of that punk world along with our rock heroes.

The drive wasn't that long but it was long enough that Philip fell asleep on my lap and the chatter in the car quieted. As the sun coughed above us and the night sky withered away, we arrived at Philip's house. We dragged ourselves out of David's car and waved goodbye, hiking up the hill toward Philip's front door. He lived in a true full-size Swiss chalet type of house on the top of a hill overlooking the Long Island Sound. It was white with blue baby-doll shutters and luscious spears of a green-bladed lawn out front. It looked straight out of *The Sound of Music*.

We went through the back door to the kitchen. No one was awake. We snickered and tiptoed up three flights to the attic and quietly opened the door to his room. I started feeling overwhelmed with fatigue, so I put my bag down near his bed and flopped down. Suddenly, the back of my head flared with a sharp pain. I had hit it on the bed frame. I quickly sat up. My head ached. Philip giggled and rubbed it. I had forgotten that we both had to sleep on a bed made for a munchkin who no doubt lived in this cookie-cutter house years ago.

I ended up staying in Philip's room for the next two weeks. Philip had to go to school, but Friends was on spring break—public and private schools hewed to different calendars. I stayed in his room on his bed watching TV every day. I don't know if his parents knew I was there, because no one ever came up to that attic bedroom. Maybe they were instructed to stay away—I don't know. Every morning after Philip and his sister and brother left for school, I tiptoed downstairs and, at the speed of light, took a quick shower and brushed my teeth; then I flashed back upstairs to Philip's tiny bed and turned on *The Brady Bunch*. I was always hungry, so Philip kept a stash of candy under the bed for me to munch on; then, when he got home, he would bring a sandwich up to me—feeding the alien in the closet. Actually, it was a nice break from the city, and I really didn't have to get back there anyway. I didn't have anywhere to go back to, and my father and I weren't speaking.

A few weeks later, we ended up playing our first show at CBGB opening for Teenage Jesus and the Jerks. As momentous as this felt to us, we got an even bigger shock. One of our favorite songs to play was a cover of "Re-Make/Re-Model" by Roxy Music, and as we banged into the start of it that night, we all suddenly noticed Brian Eno, one of the star members of Roxy Music, sitting a few rows back in the audience. Lori twirled around to me as she played and her eyes swung up in disbelief. Why couldn't he have shown up during a different song? It felt like Shakespeare stopping by while we were directing Hamlet in his death scene.

It turned out that the shows during those first few weeks were really well received, and Jody made arrangements for future bookings at Max's and CBGB and other clubs in the area. As we played more shows and developed a bigger following, we wrote more songs and toured up and down the East Coast. However, being homeless had become a sharp thorn in my life.

10

WITHOUT A CHIEF

I WAS STILL AT FRIENDS AND STUDYING *The Canterbury Tales* with Mr. Schwartz and taking all the other courses required of an eleventh grader, but I couldn't keep crashing at Bill's and Lori's houses.

In late May of '78—about a month after the Max's show—I was watching Yancy and we were building a fort of blankets and books in her room when Leslie came home. As I folded up the blankets and helped Yancy get ready for a bath, I mentioned my homeless world and that I wasn't even sure where I would sleep that night. Leslie grabbed a Dr Pepper from the refrigerator and sat on the sofa while I cleaned up. She was so engaging even though she was clearly exhausted from work, and she listened closely as I grumbled about my dilemma. Then, without missing a beat, she offered to let me to stay with her and Yancy for a few days; then she said that she and her ex, Joe, owned a small basement studio a few blocks from her house where I could crash while, hopefully, she mused, I might work things out with my dad.

I stayed with her and Yancy for a few nights. Then, at the end of the week, when Leslie got home from work, we walked a few blocks east to Perry Street to a town house in the middle of the block. She motioned me to follow as she unlocked a street-side gate below the front steps, which led to the basement level, then to a towering cement door. It opened into a long, narrow, cobwebbed hallway full of dust and grime and cracked clay slipping off the walls. The floor and the ceiling sloped to the side. I crept over the fissures of moldy cement—and it felt like the ceiling would fall on top of me as I moved forward. I wondered how in the world that building was still standing.

At the end of the hall, Leslie opened a smaller steel door and we walked into the basement studio, a disheveled though seemingly structured space, with a broken-down wooden counter on the right surrounding what seemed like an ancient, never-touched kitchen. It had a compact refrigerator and a sink but no stove. Behind the kitchen was a short hallway of moldy, aged concrete walls leading into a small room with a sink and toilet and a standing shower, and behind that, a tiny cement room with a small double bed and a window, with a TV hanging from the ceiling.

The main room by the front door was stacked with boxes, bags, and cartons of all kinds of things. Some were labeled "Joe" or "Leslie" or "Lovin' Spoonful." The front of the room was a wall of floor-to-ceiling windows and it looked out into the rear of the town house. There was a small backyard with two sky-high maple trees planted amid blunted patches of stale grass. Right in front of the center window stretched a long shelf along the floor in the studio, filled with record albums. It expanded across the length of the room. I reached down and picked up an album: *Abbey Road*. There was some writing on it but I couldn't make out what it said.

I looked around and a shaky smile came to me. "My own place," I thought to myself. My own pad.

Except it wasn't.

During the next few weeks, Lori moved in. We were roommates now and at sixteen, I was feeling very grown-up. Philip and David were there on the weekends. Of course Philip and I took the small bedroom, though actually we spent most of our time in the shower. On any given night, Lori and David and their friends crashed in the main room, where there was a pretty decent stereo system and we played rock 'n' roll albums constantly. I even fantasized about Joe coming here and secretly listening to the Lovin' Spoonful's "Daydream" or "Do You Believe in Magic."

Perry Street, as we all started to call the place, became a hotbed for all sorts of brash, upcoming punk rockers on the scene: all the guys in the Blessed, Kid Congo from the Cramps, and, through word from the Mumps, a bunch of L.A. rockers—all the girls in the Plungers (Hellin Killer, Trudie Trudie, and Mary Rat), K. K. Barrett from the Screamers, Pleasant Gehman from Screamin' Sirens—they all stayed there, and we partied and danced through the possibilities and perplexities of our lives. Many people had jobs during the day but returned at night, usually late, and often to sleep off a drunken haze.

One night, it was lightly snowing outside, and David, Philip, Lori, Bill, and I were huddled in the small cement bedroom watching *Deadman's Curve*, about the car crash that crippled Jan Berry of the famous rock duo Jan and Dean. Although we were engrossed in the movie, when it began to detail Jan's injuries and pain, we started to get depressed, so we decided to go to Max's.

David had his mother's car with him, and we all climbed in the back to head across town. It was still snowing lightly. When he drove up to Eighteenth Street and Eighth Avenue and turned to go east, for some reason, we found ourselves chanting "Go Jan go! Go Jan go!" inspired by the movie.

Except that movie ended in a car crash.

David pressed the gas pedal to the floor and took off, but just then, the traffic light turned red as a taxicab was sailing down Seventh Avenue. At that very moment we T-boned the side of the cab and spiraled to the next corner. Luckily, we came to a stop just before flipping over. We were stunned, and for a moment, completely silent.

We shakily peered out at the side of the car by our seats. Everything seemed all right, though David discovered that the front left headlight had sheared completely off. After making sure every one of us was okay, he quickly started the car up and took off down the avenue, sneaking off onto a side street to get away from the taxi. But a few minutes later, we all turned around and saw it barreling after us. We hit another red light, and when we stopped, the taxi veered in front and boxed us in. The driver burst out of his car in a fury. He raced to David's window screaming madly. I didn't understand a word he was saying but it didn't matter. He scared us to death.

David tried to calm the guy down, and after a few minutes, he gave the guy his license as collateral for a $400 payment David would get to him the next day.

We were all completely freaked. David carefully drove the car to Max's, where we lunged into a booth at the back of the club. I held onto Philip as the waitress came over.

"What'll you all have?" she asked.

"Black Russians!" David exclaimed. "All around," he said. "It's a Black Russian night."

We were still shaking. Then Philip piped up.

"Actually, I'll have a cyanide," he said, and a smile sneakily painted itself above his chin.

We looked at each other. A moment passed, then we all fell back in the booth and started laughing. We were okay. It was all okay.

The next day, David decided that, in honor of our near escape and inspired by Jan and Dean's real world tragedy, he would take on "Jan David Cruel" as his stage name. Then he and Philip hunkered down at Philip's house and wrote "Christmas Weather":[1]

I pushed my way through town
Tried to nail a cabbie down
None of them would take me for a ride

Red snow is on the ground
My swift steps don't make a sound
I can't wait 'til I get inside

If I could just have some cyanide
Swear to God I wouldn't cry and I'd
Sit by the window where no one could see me
I'd be so quiet that wouldn't believe me

Outside was Christmas weather
A thousand years since we been together
I was looking for the legendary warmth

The crowd moves with simulation
Green lights, the situation
It's purely function given form

---

1 David told his parents, upon their return home "that I'd parked the car in the train station lot. It had snowed ('Outside was Christmas weather . . . '); in fact, the car was buried in snow. Then the snow was plowed . . . and of course the plow was painted yellow. *That* was how the headlight got sheared off and why it had taxi-yellow paint on it."

My cigarettes have oozed with the table
I'll sit up straight as long as I am able
I think I'll have an accident tonight

You're not as pretty as you are in the dark
Nonetheless you've left your mark
There's just one thing that could affect me right
(And that's . . .)

If I could just have some cyanide
Swear to God I wouldn't cry and I'd
Sit by the window where no one could see me
I'd be so quiet that you wouldn't believe me

I'm a victim of a great mistake
What difference could one glass make
If I can still make it across the floor

I'll drive you home, all right
I'll stop at every traffic light
But I don't love you anymore

If I could just have some cyanide
Swear to God I wouldn't cry and I'd
Sit by the window where no one could see me
I'd be so quiet that you wouldn't believe me[2]

. . .

ALTHOUGH I WAS GRATEFUL to have a place to live, Perry Street could get chaotic and tiring. Chaos certainly feeds energy to perform and achieve, but sometimes it just breaks you down. There were times when I needed to walk down the block away from the Perry Street studio, just to escape that disorder. I usually ended up at the corner phone booth and called my mom. I did this every Friday. I wanted her to know I was

---

2 From "Christmas Weather," the B side of the single "Channel 13," released by Ork Records, 1979. Music and lyrics by David Scharff and Philip Shelley.

all right, but more than that, I needed to connect with her, and with something other than Perry Street. From time to time, even Andrew visited and brought me a bag of groceries. I still watched Yancy and made fifty dollars a week, and even though Leslie wasn't charging me for the studio, money was tight, so I was very thankful for Andrew's generosity. Although, it kind of seemed as if he was checking up on me, or on where I was and if I was safe. Maybe he was.

My final on *The Canterbury Tales* did not go well. Mr. Schwartz eyed me impatiently and with significant agitation as he marched past me during the noontime exam the following week. He stopped and moaned as he looked upon my empty page. I knew "The Miller's Tale"—I knew it cold. But something just wasn't making it through me to that page of the exam. He wanted to know what Alison does with her lover, Nicholas, and her husband, John. And I knew. But it wasn't coming. I was tired. I was playing too many roles, bouncing from pigeonhole to pigeonhole and feeling confused. Schoolwork barely registered in my consciousness. And it didn't help that I was drinking too much.

11

A BUSY MAN

IN LATE AUGUST OF '78, WE WERE SET TO OPEN for the Mumps at CBGB. When we arrived for the sound check that afternoon, the place was uncomfortably quiet, except for the bartenders clanging glasses, stacking beers, and popping corks. When I opened the door, the sunlight flooded the walls, then disappeared just as quickly as the door closed on the silent cool of the empty nightclub.

I stood at the back for a moment, watching Lance and Kristian onstage. Kristian bounced across the keys as Rob jumped onstage and plugged into his amp. They all tuned up, and their disorganized sounds filled the dark room. Antone and I lugged our equipment toward the stage as Lance and Kristian began working through a song. I grabbed my snare and my ride cymbal from Antone and walked next to the stage. Kevin climbed up and plugged his bass in, clipping out convoluted, distorted sounds from his amp. I saw Paul climb up and jump behind his drums after grabbing a kiss from a fresh-faced auburn-haired girl following him. I guess that made sense. We had only dated a few times. But my heart twisted a little at seeing them together.

The show with the Mumps went great, and by this time we had started to have a following of our own. It was very motivating and exciting, even though for some reason, I found myself trying to keep everything at arm's length.

Lori and I were still living at Perry Street, and now that summer was upon us, Philip and David had essentially moved in. Jody was there a lot too, keeping a watchful eye on all of us, and as school finished for David and Philip in Mamaroneck, we all were free to take off. Although we did a lot of gigs at Max's and CB's, as midsummer blew in, we ventured to the Hot Club in Philadelphia.

We had to travel there in Antone's van because both bodies and equipment had to get there. Climbing into the back of his van was an adventure. I had to sit between two guitar amps covered in blankets to help secure them for the ride. My drum set and Bill's keyboard were stacked carefully against the van wall, and Lori, David, and Philip crawled into the other side: human buffers for the equipment. If any of it fell, it would be caught by them and saved. Most of our equipment was borrowed and had to be saved. Didn't matter if there was no one left alive to play it.

There was not a single window in the back of that van, and the New York summer heat sucked up every bead of our oxygen and strength throughout the trek south on I-95. Bill and Antone sat up front and kept the windows open so we could get some relief, though it was minuscule.

Having a blast at the Hot Club. (PHOTO BY STEVE LOMBARDI)

We listened to a cassette of Antone's punk/new wave singles mixtape on his tape recorder and passed around bottles of orange juice and soda, and we spent the entire ride playing the card game hearts. We had all become addicted and played it constantly. Philip won more than he should have but he couldn't help it. It made me laugh every time he took the trick over every one of us. It was almost inhuman how often he won.

About two hours later, we arrived at the Hot Club and unpacked our equipment. The place was small and the stage was shaped like a triangle jutting out from one corner. It was frighteningly tiny. We all got on the stage but it was tight, a real squeeze. My drum set actually teetered at the edge and I feared if I hit the tom too hard, the drum would fly smack onto the floor.

But the sound check went fine. Afterward, we broke down our gear and moved it to the floor. We were opening for the British art-punk band Magazine, and as we finished, Howard Devoto and the band arrived for their check. Jody, Lori, and I grabbed our bags to head back to the hotel, but I couldn't find Philip. I checked backstage upstairs and he wasn't there, nor was he in the bathroom. Everyone had climbed into the van to get going, but I couldn't find Philip.

After a few minutes I heard screaming and clapping from the side room of the club. I ventured through the doorway and found a bar. A group of heavyset loggers sat there chugging beers and tossing Phillies baseball hats into the air. They cheered at the television hanging above the bar. I looked up. A Phillies game. They must've won, I thought. I look around and noticed Philip in the corner by the kitchen. When I got closer to him, I saw he was drinking a scotch. I looked at my watch. It was four thirty in the afternoon.

"What are you doing?" I asked. He downed the shot of scotch and got up, grabbing his bag.

"Nothing," he said. "Let's go."

"No," I said. "Why were you here by yourself drinking at four in the afternoon? What's going on?" I asked.

He ignored me and kept walking.

Tricks.

I was worried again.

When we got back to the hotel, we collapsed in the room. We all shared one room because that's all we could afford. Even though we were being paid for shows now, all of it went to covering band expenses, and even then it wasn't enough. Thankfully, Bill and Jody carried the outstanding weight of many expenses, while we kept borrowing equipment.

Lori jumped in the shower and I laid back on the bed by the window. Bill switched on the TV while David and Philip huddled in the corner. My eyes watered a little as I fought sleep and gazed unevenly at the ceiling. I turned over toward David and Philip and noticed David digging something out of his pocket and looking closely at it with Philip. They were huddled like two kids who'd discovered a dead turtle on the back porch and were trying to wake it up.

I sat up and grabbed a deck of cards from my bag and dealt out a round of hearts on the bed. After Bill settled on *Hawaii Five-O* on the TV, he came over and sat on the bed to play. When I finished dealing, David and Philip popped over and sat on the bed with us. David carried with him the Bible. He set it down in the middle of the game. It had five white powder lines on it. Cocaine.

I had seen it a few times before but had never tried it. David and Philip were really fired up about it, and after they grabbed their cards they each rolled up a dollar bill and sniffed up one of the lines. Then they handed it to Bill, who snorted one, and then to me. I lifted my head as I watched Jody walk to the door and leave to meet up with Antone. This was not her scene. I followed her out the door with my eyes, then looked back at the lines on the Bible. The guys were busy starting the game and laughing. They pushed my cards to me with the Bible and the white line on it. I put down my first card, then took the rolled dollar bill and sniffed the line. It felt like it was ripping up my sinuses but it didn't hurt. I looked at the guys and we all started giggling. After a few minutes, I felt like I ruled that game, that I ruled everything.

The show at the Hot Club went great, even greater than I'd thought it would and I expect the coke we had done had a lot to do with it. At least it helped our perception of it. We could only stay long enough to watch part of Magazine's set, and we couldn't crash at the hotel either, because both Antone and Jody had to be at work in the morning. We had to get going.[1] After our set, we piled the equipment and ourselves into the back

---

1 Philip recalls talking the pissed-off bartender into giving us a case of beer for the ride home and that the Hot Club owner ended up managing the Bloodless Pharaohs for a while.

of the van. I fell asleep on the ride back and maybe everyone else did, I don't know.[2] Antone dropped us at Perry Street at around 3 a.m. and took the equipment back with him. He had to get home.

The next day when I got up and stumbled to the kitchen in the front room, I saw there were about fifteen people splayed out across the floor. The place had become a punk rock flophouse. I looked at my watch. It was 3 p.m. I wandered to the small refrigerator and opened it. There were two Pepsis on the bottom shelf; the two upper shelves were covered with Budweisers. I had to get to the store. I grabbed a Pepsi. Then, as I shut the refrigerator, the front door suddenly slammed open.

Joe Butler stood there, his eyes in flames, screaming.

"Get out!"

I stood there paralyzed, holding the Pepsi bottle to my open mouth. Everyone jumped off the floor. The sun blasted the room through the windows, and even the naked bodies rising up were warmed by it. But not for long.

Turns out someone had been stealing valuable records autographed to Joe by John Lennon, the Beatles, and the Rolling Stones as well as albums signed by Lovin' Spoonful—and they were selling them. He was livid. He demanded we all get out of his space immediately. I quickly approached him and apologized. I told him I would do whatever I could to fix the situation. Here was this icon of 1960s rock 'n' roll who had allowed me to stay here and someone had purloined his private property. I was mortified.

Joe Butler didn't want to hear my apology. He stood there at attention, his arms folded, ready to point his AK-47 at us—if he had one. He demanded every single one of us get out right then and there or he would call the police. We all packed up everything we could find while Joe stood there, threatening each one of us through his raging breath. We exited in single file through the disintegrating basement hallway, carrying everything we could handle with us.

Perry Street was over.

---

2   David says: "Driving there and back was so tight, I was wedged between an amp and the back door. If Antone hit the gas too hard, I had to use my meager strength to hold the amps at bay and not get crushed!" And at one point on the ride back to New York, Philip recalls Antone looking in the rearview mirror shouting, "Oh shit! It's the police, and they're not singing 'Roxanne'!"

After everyone took off to their homes or to the local coffee shop, Lori and I stood in front of the town house with two suitcases and three trash bags. While Lori sat on the neighboring stoop, I went to the phone booth at the corner. I dialed Mom.

"You know, baby," she said to me, "it's time to go home. It's time to work things out with your father."

"He doesn't want to, Mom."

"Yes, he does, honey," she said. "He loves you." I gulped some air, then kissed her through the phone and said goodbye.

I spent that night at Lori's place in Brooklyn. Reluctantly, I finally called my dad. He wasn't home, but Jane was, and so was MB. They urged me to come home too. I looked around Lori's house. The TV blasted *Days of Our Lives* while her aunt stirred a pot of what smelled like sumptuous spaghetti sauce on the stove inside their miniature kitchen and snapped at the TV through the cigarette dangling between her lips. I guess they were right.

The next day, I dragged my suitcase and a trash bag of clothes to the subway and straggled home to SoHo. I remember sitting in the subway car watching a guy performing as a mime then passing his hat around for money. He wore a striped sailor shirt and a black beret. He had a frizzled goatee and large, empty black eyes. He didn't say one word but begged everyone through his shattered gaze. I couldn't give him anything, and he made me feel dejected. That was his job I guess.

When I got back to my building on Wooster Street, I called for the freight elevator and dragged my bags onto it. I pushed the elevator handle to 4 and headed up. When I opened the door, my dad was standing right there. Had he been waiting for me? He was rarely ever home. He just stood there when the elevator doors opened. I pulled my suitcase into the hall.

"Hi," I said to him.

"Hi," he replied. "I was waiting for the elevator."

He slipped past me and got on. I turned around to him. Towering, with a Kennedy haircut and hectic blue eyes, he never stopped. For anyone.

"I understand you're back," he said.

"Yeah," I replied. He nodded and I tried to see a smile on him. I pinched my eyelids.

"I left a note on your bed," he said. "I have a meeting."

Then he closed the elevator doors. I picked up my suitcase and pushed open the front door of the loft. I dragged myself to my room, threw my bags on the bed, and fell onto my pillow. I grabbed Dad's note.

1) Don't forget to put the dishes in the dishwasher.
2) Your bathroom needs a wipe-down.
3) Move the books from the hallway shelves to the living room.
4) Dinner tonight with the Everlys

My head dropped back and I stared at the ceiling. A busy man, I thought to myself. A busy man.

12

HYPNOTIC

DURING THE SUMMER OF '78, we had played shows almost weekly in the city as we continued to build our fan base. We'd started to get some good reviews in local New York papers such as the *New York Rocker* and the *Village Voice*. Inveterate rock 'n' roll reviewer Robert Christgau at the *Village Voice* called us "rather more popish, featuring two of the Erasers' roadies," and the *New Musical Express* called us the "Teen Tyros of the New Music Scene." And in August, a profile of us came out in *Melody Maker* titled "Teaching Practice."[1] We were opening a lot for out-of-town bands at Max's because Crowley knew we were anxious to play and would do it for low pay, and he wanted to promote us. As fall arrived, we found ourselves playing nearly three gigs every month. We were there. We were sensing ourselves as not just a fan-fueled band but a real band that could make its own mark. We were doing it on our own. And we believed we could make it.

Twelfth grade at Friends started unceremoniously for me. Bill was a year older, so he had graduated and was now attending NYU, studying art history. David and Philip had graduated high school as well. David was at NYU too, but Philip hadn't started college yet, and Lori and Jody were busy working.

Because it was senior year, I had the chance to choose my own courses, and I found myself taking as much of what Mr. Schwartz was teaching as possible. More often than not, though, I was in the school cafeteria located

---

1   Harry Doherty, "Teaching Practice," *Melody Maker*, August 18, 1979.

in the basement, drinking tea and reading, or, even more likely, sleeping. Burning the candles at both ends was taking its toll and I kept lighting the match. The tension between academics and rock 'n' roll was constantly gripping me.

One day when I was sweating over a study sheet for physics in the cafeteria, Mr. Schwartz came in and approached me. I looked up, trying desperately to remain calm.

An exact Gregory Peck look-alike from *To Kill a Mockingbird*, Mr. Schwartz was incessantly awash in papers, books, and folders. I never saw him at ease: He was always "on" and always, when asked, spouting Latin and Greek texts—his specialty. I adored him.

"What are you doing, young lady?" he said, his expression one of ominous dismay.

"Studying, sir," I replied calmly . . . oh so calmly.

He sat down at the table across from me. My hands quivered on my knees.

"I mean—what are you doing with your studies?" he came back.

"What do you mean?" I asked.

"You're near failing everything and you got a C- on the *Canterbury Tales* exam," he enumerated. I gulped. That was news.

"What is going on? You're smarter than that and you know it," he asserted, and not in a nice way.

I was messing up. I knew that. It was really difficult keeping it all going at the same time. Even though I was back in school, we were still rehearsing a lot, and Bill and Philip were bringing in new songs, shows were being scheduled—somewhere deep behind the crazed flash swimming through all of us, we were trying to succeed. I wasn't entirely aware of it: Maybe the others were, I didn't know. More than anything, though, it felt like I was on a flatbed truck racing down a deserted road of confusion. And I couldn't get off even if I wanted to, and I didn't.

Mr. Schwartz got up and stuffed his workload into his briefcase as he grabbed his empty teacup and gave me one last look.

"Get better at this," he said, piercing me with his eyes.

"Yes, sir."

He walked away as I dropped my head into my hands.

. ● .

IN LATE OCTOBER, WE OPENED FOR THE KNOW at Max's. The Know was a band created by Gary Valentine, previous bass player for Blondie. Although Gary had written Blondie's first single, "X Offender," he'd eventually had a falling-out with the band and left.

Gary had bushy brown hair and a confident step about him. He looked smart and silvery coy. All the girls adored him. This was our first gig with him, and it really excited us because the Know sounded, in many ways, how we wanted to sound.

That night after we played our opening set and ran upstairs to recover, sweating and parched, I heard a pounding up the stairs behind us and a booming laugh enter the room. When I pulled the towel off of my head Jimmy Destri was standing there. I certainly knew him from the Blondie records. He was the keyboard player and had written one of my favorite songs, "A Shark in Jets Clothing."

He stood there raising his beer to us, smiling bigger than I'd ever seen anyone smile in my life. I was briefly speechless. He was a little taller than me, stick-thin like many rock 'n' rollers, but with a muscular build and tan, moist-looking skin. He was stunningly handsome, far more so than he looked on the back of the *Plastic Letters* album. His hair was black and dropped over his forehead like James Dean's. He had full lips and bright, feverish eyes in a face that looked like it had been born to a hardy rancher and his wife on a farm outside of Paris. He stood there in tight white jeans and a black T-shirt, with a slight self-awareness of how striking he was but also with a very young, almost childlike giddiness about everything around him. He was a photographer's dream, I thought. And standing next to Debbie Harry, he looked exactly that way on their albums.

"Absolutely phenomenal show!" he belted as he plowed in and sat down between Bill and David.

David immediately started talking to him about the show. Jimmy said he really liked the set, particularly the song "The Quake." He asked us how we'd all gotten together and how we'd come to play our instruments. Then he came over to me and Lori and asked how we'd gotten our rhythm section together. He thought our all-female setup was a great idea.

All energy, all himself. (PHOTO BY MAUREEN DONALDSON/GETTY IMAGES)

After a few minutes, Jimmy grabbed us all to go downstairs and watch the Know. He was a big fan even though he and Gary had had a strained relationship when Gary was in Blondie. Jimmy was all energy, all wired. When we got downstairs to the bar, the Know were tuning and prepping. The place was jam-packed and the crowd was eager. Gary had a strong following from his days in Blondie but had started developing his own as well.

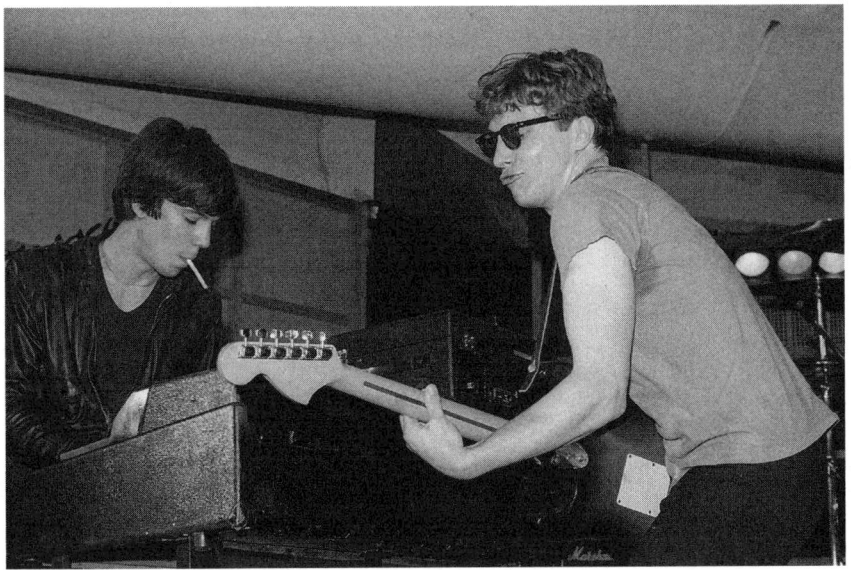

Jimmy and Gary playing it out. (PHOTO BY STEVE LOMBARDI)

Jimmy pulled us all into a booth by the front windows and bought us a round of White Russians. As Gary started singing, I noticed Jimmy talking heatedly to David and Philip. I couldn't hear what he was saying over the music, but he was dancing in his seat and laughing. We didn't know him, but he had taken a sudden, forceful, almost panicked interest in us. He frantically smoked Parliament cigarettes, offering them to the whole table. I turned away and watched Gary onstage, wondering. Then I grabbed Philip's hand. And I noticed Jimmy watching me as I did.

13

PHANTASM

THROUGH OCTOBER AND NOVEMBER, Jimmy came to all our shows. He also hung out with us afterward, buying us drinks and eventually handing out drugs to everyone—mostly cocaine. Coke was really expensive, but Jimmy, rock star in residence at the time, always had a few packets of it on him. And he loved to share it.[1]

At this time, the Mudd Club had become the hot place to go to after shows had finished at the nightclubs. It was located farther downtown on White Street, and it was run by Steve Mass, Diego Cortez, and well-known nightclub veteran Anya Phillips. Always at midnight through the week, there were crowds of punk rockers, fashion designers, models, and musicians lining the streets to get in. It was a reaction to the uptown clubs, such as Studio 54, where clubgoers always arrived in limos. The Mudd Club was for the young, the punky, the neoteric.

After one gig, when we played at Max's opening for the Troggs, Jimmy grabbed a cab and took us all to the Mudd Club. While in the cab he stretched out his wrist to me with a line of coke and a rolled-up hundred-dollar bill. The taxi bounced over the potholed streets wildly but Jimmy held his wrist steady as a rock as he handed me the bill. I sniffed up the coke and handed the bill back to him. But he wouldn't take it.

"Keep it," he mouthed. I looked over at Philip, shocked.

---

1   Philip recalls Jimmy bonding with us by buying us all flasks of Jack Daniel's and tromping around town, and one time, Jimmy getting thrown down the stairs at Max's by the bouncer ("Do you know who I am???"). David remembers that I helped Jimmy when he was thrown down the stairs and foresaw us getting together.

When we arrived, the cab pulled up right in front of the club and Jimmy quickly jumped out, madly pulling us with him. He tossed a twenty to the driver and marched through the front door, busting in front of a line of hundreds waiting to get in. He turned to the bouncer:

"They're with me," he announced.

And we were ushered in without question. There were so many bodies dancing, jumping, singing, kicking, drinking, and shouting, the walls of the place literally swelled and ballooned out into the streets. Jimmy bounced up the stairs and we trailed after him—five little ducklings following their mother across the road.

It was slightly less busy upstairs and there was a bar at the front. We ambled over, watching the circus of performing drinkers and swingers swaying through the crowd. The Ramones' "Rockaway Beach" blasted from the speakers, and the walls were covered in graffiti—art, I learned later, by Keith Haring. I didn't realize much then. I barely saw happenings around me. I was just there. Rootless.

Seeking a place of non-movement, of stagnation, I stayed at the bar to just watch. My mom had taught me when I was younger that the best thing to do when we were stuck somewhere like a bus station or on a grocery store line was to "people watch." I wasn't stuck, but I craved a twinkling of stillness. I stood quietly and watched.

A moment later, an older woman approached me. She had long blonde hair and was a little overweight—in a regal, understated way. She exuded a definite monarchical quality. She was not to be doubted. She was not to be taken for granted.

"Having a good time?" she asked me.

"Yes," I said. "How about you?"

"Well, I've been waiting for Mick but he hasn't shown." I looked at her again. Mick? Jagger? I thought to myself.

"Excuse me, but are you Marianne Faithfull?" I asked in amazement. She downed her drink and nodded.

"Yes, you new here?"

"It's my first time." I replied. She nodded and looked around.

"Don't make it your last," she said and smiled assuredly with a self-possession I didn't see anywhere else in that club.

Suddenly, Jimmy grabbed my hand and dragged me to the back. I looked for Philip but he wasn't around. Had he left?

Jimmy pulled me into one of the bathrooms and took out one of those small packets and poured out four lines of cocaine on the counter next to the sink. I looked past him and there was a young woman with striped purple and green hair sitting on the toilet. These were the Mudd Club bathrooms: transgender, unisex, open. The striped-haired girl looked up at me and smiled through her shiny black lips. I nodded.

"Here," Jimmy said, and handed me another rolled-up hundred-dollar bill. I took it, leaned over, and sniffed. Then I handed the bill back to him.

"No," he said. "Have another." I sniffed up another one. Then he took the bill and snorted the other two lines. The striped-haired girl got up and flushed.

"Hey, can I have one?"

She sounded so far away from us—a phantom.

Jimmy grabbed up the packet and pushed me out the door. Outside of the bathroom he jammed me up into the wall.

"Come home with me," he said. I looked at him. His eyes were tight, with red lines streaming into the corners. He wasn't smiling. He was dead serious.

"Come on, baby," he said and he started kissing my neck and running his hands down between my legs. I stiffened. Before I could answer, David appeared and said Philip was looking for me. I squeaked away from Jimmy, whom I saw hand David his coke packet as I went to find Philip.

I crept through the club but I couldn't stop thinking about Jimmy. He was clearly very drunk and stoned, so his offer was obviously a joke. From what I had read, I knew he was in a relationship with Joan Jett, but as I understood it, she was on tour with her band, the Runaways. He was just lonely and plastered. He would be fine the next day, I figured. I found Philip by the front door and we decided to hop a subway to my house and stay there for what remained of the night. I kept reminding myself, as I sat on the jerking train ride home, that Jimmy would be fine the next day.

· · ·

ON THE SECOND SATURDAY IN DECEMBER, we were at Max's opening for the Fast. Because the Fast were a huge icon of the downtown punk scene—three racy dark young brothers with shining tortured black hair from Brooklyn—they had an intensely loyal New York fan base, and luckily, their fans liked our band.

I had a final in French the following Monday, so I found myself hunkered down in the dressing room upstairs chugging a beer and munching on French fries while I dug into my textbook, *French for Reading*. Luckily, Lori hung around quizzing me on verbs.

"To wash?" Lori asked, blowing smoke through the words.

"*Lavage!*" I replied with a smile.

David came upstairs to tell us it was time for the sound check and I asked him where Philip was but he didn't know. When we got downstairs onto the stage, Lori plugged in her bass, Bill appeared and ran his fingers across the keys, and I checked the tone of my snare and my bass drum. While we tuned, Jody came up and said she hadn't found Philip, except that he had been with us lugging in the equipment earlier.

We waited for another twenty minutes, then dispersed. Since we didn't have to move the equipment off of the stage, because we were going on first, I immediately dashed back upstairs to dig into my French. School was closing for the holidays after my exam on the following Monday. I had to do well on the final or I would have to go back in during the break to retake it, and that would be disastrous. We had a big show coming up with the Know at Hurrah a few days before Christmas.

But when I jumped into the dressing room, I came to a bracing stop. There was Philip, passed out on the floor. I shook him.

"Hey, Philip! Wake up!" I frantically whispered.

Just then, Lori and David came in. I bent over Philip's face and kissed him. Suddenly, I was hit with a huge cloud of vodka fumes and I immediately sat back up. He was out.

Luckily, Philip woke up a little while later. He was groggy and slightly hungover but he said he could do the show. I sat close to him and never left his side. He said he was okay and I heard him as I rubbed his back and gave him some coffee. But I didn't believe him.

It was getting hard to know Philip. He had started to move away from all of us in a way that didn't say he wasn't part of the band, but rather said that he was having trouble staying conscious. It was getting to the point where he was drunk or wasted nearly all of the time and, yes, that is and was a natural outgrowth of the rock 'n' roll world. Getting wasted on alcohol or drugs seemed to be a necessity in order to achieve in that arena. Just as you have to be able to parallel park in order to get a driver's license, you have to get sufficiently wasted, on a regular basis, in order to gain the license to be onstage and perform rock 'n' roll. Many people can handle it. Most can't.

The show with the Fast went okay. It wasn't one of our best, but thankfully, our fans were very forgiving. After the Fast's set ended, we all went to the restaurant to have some food. I was hoping it would help Philip to get something in his stomach.

As we ordered burgers and chili, Jimmy suddenly appeared. He said he had come in late but caught the last part of our set. David mentioned how it wasn't our best, but Jimmy didn't seem to notice. We hungrily worked on our cheeseburgers and fries as Jimmy grabbed a chair and sat down at the end of the booth. He smiled and grabbed a fry off of my plate. He said he had been thinking about our song "The Quake" a lot and had been working on it on his synthesizer. He was in the studio with Blondie, recording their next record, and he said he'd been playing around with our song on his off time. Jimmy then said that he wanted to record it with us, that he had been talking with Terry Ork about producing a single of two of our songs. I stopped chewing and looked up at the guys. David looked like he might choke on his burger. He roughly swallowed.

"That is a great idea!" he exclaimed, grabbing Jimmy's hand and shaking it. He looked at the rest of us.

"What do you think, guys?"

We were amazed. Everyone except Philip—he nodded to David but kept his mouth full of burger and ketchup. He continued nodding, though.

Later that night, as we loaded the instruments into Antone's van, David and Bill, thrilled over Jimmy's interest, started talking about ways to make "The Quake" work in the studio and busily talked with Jimmy about when we would do the record. They really wanted to know what Terry Ork[2] was saying about it and us.

Philip hung back, sitting on the curb, waiting. He was pretty wiped. After David and Jimmy finished talking, David went to get his car and pulled up in front of the club. It was nearly 4 a.m. and everyone else had

---

2 Manager of Television and Richard Hell, owner of Ork Records, producer of punk and new wave acts. The box collection of Ork's recordings was nominated for two Grammys in 2017. In the 2013 film *CBGB*, Ork was portrayed by Johnny Galecki.

left. Philip climbed in the back of the car, curling into a deep sleep. David waited for me to join them but I decided not to go. Philip could sleep it off, and I had to get home to study. Monday was the exam. David took off and I grabbed my bag and walked toward the subway. Suddenly, Jimmy appeared next to me.

"Where ya goin'?" he asked.

I laughed. I don't know why. I was nervous.

"Home," I said.

"Why don't you come with me instead?" he suggested and grabbed my arm as we neared the corner.

I looked at him. He was as handsome as the first day I'd met him. I pulled my arm back. I didn't know what to think. I was with Philip.

"I have to get home," I said.

He grabbed my arm again and pulled me into him.

"You should come with me," he said. Then he leaned in and kissed me for a very long time. I trembled.

It was so easy to be drawn into him. He was absolutely gorgeous and planning to help my band record a single and he was a major rock star in the making. What was my problem? The best thing about being sixteen years old is that you live in the moment, every single day and night, without awareness of the moment ahead of you or the moment behind you. And I knew that, as Jimmy wrapped his fingers around my heart. That eternal present, however, is also the problem. For that instant, it didn't capture me. But just for that instant.

Finally, I pulled away.

"I can't," I said, and ran down the street. I had to get home.

· ● ·

SURPRISINGLY, MY EXAM IN FRENCH went much better than I'd thought it would. Or at least, that's how I felt. Although I don't know if my French teacher agreed.

When I left the classroom I went downstairs to the cafeteria in the basement to get some tea. I sat down at the table in the back near the teachers' lounge and put my head down. I was really worn-out. I didn't fall asleep, I just turned off.

The kitchen and cafeteria staff were shutting down for the Christmas break. There weren't many other students down there because most of them usually hung out in the back courtyard, smoking and gossiping. That world was for the cool kids and I was, even after over three years at Friends, not one of them. Even though I was in a band and playing regularly while trying to keep up my studies, I was still an outcast. It may have been because I always wore black and kept to myself, hanging with my rock 'n' roll friends far outside of school—I don't know. But life at school was a hook I had to hang onto if I was going to get beyond it.

As I drank my tea, postponing going home, Mr. Schwartz appeared. He sat across from me and put his bursting case full of scholarly papers down on the table.

"You did better."

"On the Dante exam?" I asked. He nodded.

"I knew you could. Although your analysis of the deeper allegory was a little—"

"What?" I asked.

"Thin," he replied. "But," he continued, putting on his gloves, "good enough".

"Thank you," I said. I choked a little as I took a sip of my Lipton.

"I still expect better, much better," he reminded me as he stood up.

"I know."

He turned, buttoned his coat, grabbed his bag, and started walking away.

"Merry Christmas," he imparted as he turned the corner to the door.

"Merry Christmas, sir."

14

SURGE

TOWARD THE END OF DECEMBER, WE PLAYED at the nightclub Hurrah. Although Hurrah had been around since 1976, this was the first time we had dared to venture uptown since we'd started playing. We were opening for the Know again, which, by that point, we just loved doing, and Jody, who was one of the Know's biggest fans, had started moonlighting for them as their roadie.

When we arrived that first afternoon, hauling our equipment into Hurrah was a surreal experience. The club was on Sixty-Second Street, a world away from our downtown haunts, and it was across the street from Lincoln Center, where the giants of the classical music and operatic worlds had pounded out their arias and symphonies for half a century. I remember standing on the street in front of Hurrah looking at the crowds streaming into Lincoln Center, thinking about how different each of us was in the kind of music we were making, and why.

We entered through a long hallway, then continued through big light pink doors that opened to a mirrored, zigzagging entranceway into the main room. The space inside was vast and open, with spotlights across the ceiling. I remember standing in the middle of the room as the rest of the group dragged in their amps and equipment and saying to myself, "Is this a fucking disco?"

The bar stretched across the far wall, and above it were what looked like television screens, or video monitors, as I later learned. What were they for?

The stage was in the corner. I wandered over to it. It was bigger than at CB's or Max's, and it stretched across the back wall. Hurrah was a rock club. I knew about its history, but I was still perplexed. The big round floor, the spotlights above, the stage set off to the corner—it just kept feeling like a disco to me.

Antone and the guys brought the equipment over to the stage and started setting up. I was helping lift my bass drum and my snare onto the back when suddenly the video monitors above the bar started streaming a Clash video. Antone told us this wasn't a trendy disco like Studio 54 or Xenon—it was a new wave dance rock video club. DJs were spinning the music we knew and loved from new indie bands like the B52s, Bush Tetras, the Fleshtones, and the Contortions along with music of the past from Presley, the Stones, and Bowie. It was the true culmination of the sounds and style of a rock disco.

But it wasn't a "disco" disco.

A few hours later, after our sound check, we settled into another room across the club from the stage. This was the dressing room. Lori sat down for a smoke and Philip and David headed out to get something to eat. Jody had disappeared—probably to the land of the Know. I sat down next to Lori.

"What d'ya think?"

"It's cool," she said and inhaled. "It's a gig."

Suddenly the door opened and Jimmy marched in.

"Hey!" He smiled and leaned over and kissed me on the cheek. Lori lifted her left eyebrow at me. I playfully slapped her shoulder.

Jimmy lit a Parliament and urged us to join him at the bar. When we got out there the crowd was piling in and the monitors above were playing a video of the Ramones, from when they had played Hurrah the past August.

Jimmy offered us beers. I stayed close to Lori. We were going on in about a half hour and I needed to get my sticks from the dressing room and, well, I was feeling a little beleaguered. The crowd had grown larger and people were moving toward the stage for the show. I looked at Lori. She was listening to Jimmy's plans to get us into Blank Tape Studios in February, though I didn't know how that would happen since we weren't even signed to a record label yet. I put my beer on the bar and started to go. Suddenly I was pulled back.

Gigging at the Hurrah disco. (PHOTO BY MARY E. DAVIS)

"I need to talk to you after the show tonight," Jimmy said, returning my beer to me.

"Okay," I said, "but I have to get ready." I handed the beer back. He laughed and let me go. Lori caught up with me as I raced to the dressing room.

"Watch out for that one." She snickered.

When we got there, the guys were getting ready. David was putting on makeup, Philip was tuning his guitar, and Bill was—well, he was always ready to go onstage. I let Lori's warning pass, but she wasn't wrong. I had to watch out for that one.

By that time, as late '78 turned into early '79, we had become regulars on the New York club scene. We were doing a few shows every month, rehearsing regularly and working on a ton of new songs. The show at Hurrah went great and Merrill Aldighieri—Hurrah's video DJ—filmed it for the video collection. When we ran off the stage, sweating and breathless from the set, Jimmy was there to greet us. He was flying. He seemed so ecstatic for us. It was kind of odd to me to see someone so purely cheering for us. In a way, it was worrisome.

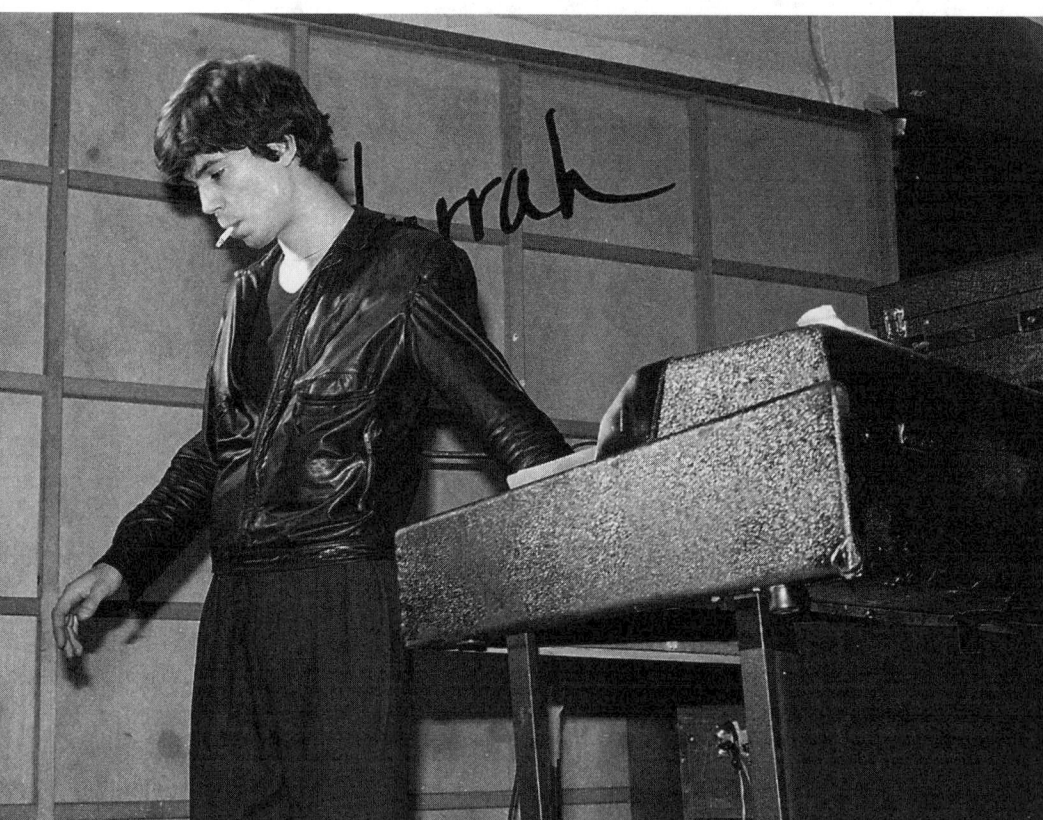

Our biggest fan—at Hurrah. (PHOTO BY STEVE LOMBARDI)

"Great show, guys!" He patted us all on the back. I twisted my head and looked at him. That guy is our biggest fan, I thought to myself.

Around midnight, after the Know had finished their last set, a bunch of us joined Jimmy at a table near the bar. He ordered us all our signature White Russians, which we drank in near silence as Jimmy suddenly raised his beer and saluted us. What was this guy doing?

"Congratulations, guys! Terry Ork has offered to sign you!"

What? After a thick moment charged with disbelief, we all screamed and jumped out of our seats. David and Bill took off and started bouncing to Iggy Pop's "Nightclubbing," which was blasting through the speakers. Lori, Jody, Antone, and Philip laughed and clapped as David and Bill marched to Iggy's description of what we were all doing: "Nightclubbing... we're nightclubbing. . . ."[1]

A few minutes later, Bill dashed to a pay phone to call his parents about the signing. David cartwheeled with giddiness but decided he and Philip would tell everyone when they got home. I wanted to call my mom but it was too late, so I thought I should tell my dad. Dimes jingled in my pocket. But then I thought Dad probably didn't remember I was even in a band.

Terry Ork was a powerhouse producer on the punk and new wave scene. He had started with the success of the band Television and Richard Hell and we could barely believe that we would now be inside of Ork's sphere. And it was all because Jimmy was interested in the band, because he thought we were a hot, evolving pop group and that we were going somewhere.

I was stunned. I'd never imagined, and likely never intended, all of this to get this far, and it was all happening so fast. We had just started playing six months previously, and I had just started on the drums a couple of months before then. I was astonished.

All the guys were swinging inside their giddiness—drunk and high and planning what we would do when we hit the record charts and headed to tour in Europe. We were flying.

At around 2 a.m., most of the band wandered out of the club—tired and weakened from the electric charge of expectation that had surged through our bodies since receiving the news. Philip had to grab a ride back to Larchmont because family had settled in for the holidays, and I

---

1   "Nightclubbing" by Iggy Pop from *The Idiot*, 1977.

knew I'd be heading south in a few days, so we kissed and promised to talk over Christmas.

I hung around a little bit longer with Jimmy and Gary and one of their closest friends, John Browner, manager of the Know and a book fanatic from Westchester who worked at Barnes & Noble. With a sharp nose and obscure pencil-thin eyes, Browner was known to Jimmy and Gary and everyone else. He was funny and cerebral, and even though he always seemed to have drugs around, Jimmy adored his wit and just hanging with him. I think everyone thought he was smart enough to take them somewhere else, beyond the grind of the rock 'n' roll world. As a result, he ended up authoring one of the first great tomes about the New York punk rock scene: *Death of a Punk*.

By that point, I was pretty drunk, and Jimmy decided to usher us all into the office behind the bar. At the desk was one of Hurrah's owners, Robert Boykin, a young, quick-witted guy with dirty-blonde hair, sweet blue eyes, and deeply rich pockets. Apparently, he was a good friend of Jimmy's and was thrilled to see us when we came in. He quickly stood up and introduced his boyfriend, a young fashion student named Marc Jacobs.

Both Jimmy and Robert took out packets of cocaine and began serving everyone lines and lines of it. It turned into an animated coke party. About an hour later, Robert moved us all back out to the bar, where we sat and drank Rémy Martin, listened to Patti Smith over the speakers, and talked.

When there were only a few of us left, Robert said he had to close up for the night, and while the bartender was cleaning up, Jimmy leaned close to me and started kissing my cheek, then biting my ear. I laughed. What was this rock star doing? He was with Blondie, for chrissakes. He was the up-and-coming producer of our band. Even more importantly, I was just a drummer—and barely a drummer at that. Why in the world was he making these moves on me?

Maybe it was the Rémy, or the coke, or the high of learning we were getting signed—I wasn't sure. But when I looked at him, I saw such a handsome, vibrant young man seizing life by its throat with so much energy. Even though he was a child, seeing the stars in the night sky for the first time, and was so raw, he was bursting—everything, every step, every choice, was original for him, and he adored it. You could see his endless rapture within every moment that he lived. It was so hard to turn away from him, and he had started to grab my heart.

We ended up going downtown to a place he was renting on Horatio Street. It was near 5 a.m. before we got there, and he was very drunk and nearly out of it, by that time. He was subletting the apartment with Nigel Harrison, Blondie's bass player, but he said that he and Nigel were just two rancorous ships in the night. Blondie was heading out on an American tour shortly, and Jimmy said he wanted me with him, before they left.

When we got there, we went upstairs to his bedroom. It was a catastrophe of tossed-off clothes and shoes and bags. He certainly seemed the typical and unapologetic rock star—always on the move, having no ties to anything. Doing laundry wasn't on his list. I remember looking around, not wanting to clean up his mess for him, but rather feeling intrigued by it all, captivated by the romance of that lack of a home, that indeterminacy, the insouciant transience of a rock star.

He tackled me. We giggled through our excited exhaustion. We made love in a very brief but explosive moment, and when I looked in his eyes, I found myself amazed that I was with him and my heart falling into his. We kissed for what felt like the rest of the night until, without warning, he collapsed into a drunken sleep—right on top of me. I couldn't move and I couldn't wake him. Even though I was afraid to bother him—he had taken in a lot of coke and alcohol—I had to pee. And I really didn't want to pee on him. I didn't want to pee on the bed either. I didn't want to pee anywhere except in the bathroom. This was our first time. But no matter what, even if this was also our last time, I had to pee. I tried to fall asleep and hoped that my body would forget what it needed for a while. But that didn't work.

"Jimmy? Jimmy?" I whispered, trying not to panic. I tried pushing him a little and tapping on his arm. But he wasn't moving. He was completely out.

Then I tried to wiggle out from under him, but that pushed his knee against my bladder. Not a good thing. I kept wiggling myself and shifting my hips and it wasn't waking him. I put my ear to his mouth. He was breathing. And even though my shifting movements weren't waking him, I was getting nowhere. And my bladder was about to burst. I breathed heavily and tried to focus myself. He would wake up in a while and I could go to the bathroom. I crossed my fingers and tried to sleep.

About four hours later, the phone rang. Jimmy's head jerked up, waking me. He looked at me and, realizing he was lying on top of me stark naked, jumped up, grabbed a shirt, and picked up the receiver. I sat up and looked between my legs. No pee. Whew. While Jimmy talked on the phone, I quickly put on my pants, grabbed my shirt, and ran for the bathroom. As I went into the hallway, I saw through the window that there was no sunlight—it was evening. I looked at my watch—6:30 p.m.—and it was Sunday. "Damn!" I said to myself. I dashed to the bathroom. I had to get home.

After I finished, I rushed to get my jacket and my bag and bounced down the stairs.

"Hey, hey! Where are you going?" Jimmy asked, running after me.

"I have to get home. It's later than I thought," I said.

As I jumped into the living room downstairs I almost banged into Nigel. He was wandering around eating some ice cream and watching the television.

"Oh, hi," I said. He swiftly turned.

"Hi." He leaned over and kissed my hand.

"Nice to meet you . . ."

He lifted his eyes up to me. He was so gentle, so unexpected. He was shorter than Jimmy but very fit, with curly light brown hair, and exquisitely dressed—very British.

"Laura Davis," I replied. "Nice to meet you too."

I smiled, then quickly raced to grab my jacket, pushing aside piles of clothes, papers, books, record albums, searching for my bag.

"Hey Nigel, that was Bruce, we have to get over there," Jimmy said at the bottom of the staircase.

Blondie were going on their second U.S. tour and their road manager, Bruce Patron, had just called to light a fire under Jimmy and Nigel.

I vaulted to the front door and raced my hands madly over all the chains and locks. Just then, Jimmy grabbed me from behind. He pushed my bag onto the floor and pulled me close and kissed me with more passion than I ever knew existed.

When he let me go, I gasped for air.

"Jimmy! Wow!" I stood back a little.

"Come with me," he begged.

"What?"

"Come with me on tour. We're back at the end of January. Come with me."

"I can't." I said.

I turned and finished sliding the locks to the side. I opened the door and raced out.

"When I get back then," he said. I looked at him. His boyish face and eyes pulled at me.

"Well," I said, "aren't we going into the studio with you when you get back?"

"Yes," he said, "but that's not all I want." I rolled my eyes. I turned and headed for the stairs.

"I'll call you when I get back!" he yelled.

I opened the front door in the lobby and quickly walked across Seventh Avenue to get home, thinking the entire time to myself, What about Philip?

A few days later, I headed down to Washington, DC, with my dad, Jane, and MB. We arrived at the home of Jane's parents—whom MB and I affectionately called Nonno and Nonna—late Christmas eve. They lived in DC, near the Washington Cathedral, in a big house surrounded by trees teeming with sprays of Concord grapes.

MB and I slept in a low-level sunroom, off the side of my dad and Jane's room, in two small cots fit for baby monkeys. It didn't matter because I was exhausted. As much as I wanted to escape the confusing pressures of Jimmy and his attention, I couldn't stop thinking about him.

He was all in my head. (PHOTO BY STEVE LOMBARDI)

15

NEVER GETTIN' OUTTA HERE

IN MID-JANUARY, WE OPENED FOR THE ERASERS at CBGB. It was bitterly cold out but that didn't faze us. We were flying high now. We weren't just fans who happened to be onstage. We weren't just a band slated to play this gig. We were recording artists and authentic. We were a real band.

Thus, weather had no place and no meaning. Winter was summer for us. The energy within each of us, and the vigor holding us together as we bounced through each gig and rehearsal, kept the warmth between us as we huddled outside of McDonald's after rehearsal, or when we all hung on the cars parked outside of CB's in the snow. Everywhere we went, the frost melted.

After our set opening for the Erasers, I went up to the bar and ordered a beer. David came over with a few of the Larchmont crowd—Ellen, Eloise, Sandra, and Robert. Ellen Kinnally was a stunning fashionista with bright hair and smoky eyes who periodically go-go danced onstage during one of our sets. She had been David's date at his prom when he graduated Mamaroneck High School. But they were just friends, because I don't think David was sure who he was then. He was gay, then he wasn't; he was straight, then he wasn't; he was bisexual, then he wasn't. He was discovering himself, and that night, he was hanging very closely with his crowd when he came over, ordered a beer, and started laughing.

"Great show, don't ya think?" he said. Ellen and Sandra jumped and danced to the Cramps song "Human Fly" coming through the speakers.

"Yeah," I said.

Suddenly, David splashed his drink all over my shirt.

"Whoa!" he screeched.

I backed away, madly grabbing napkins from the bar.

Then I looked up and Jimmy was standing there. He had tripped and fallen into David, and David had crashed into me. David was laughing even more, and he slapped Jimmy on the back. Bros. Comrades in arms. Fellow conspirators.

"Don't worry!" David said. He helped me with the napkins, now disintegrating into a mountain of cotton pulp.

"Hi," Jimmy said, looking at me.

David leaned over to Jimmy. He was a little drunk.

"Did you see the show?" he asked.

"Yes," Jimmy said looking at me. "Loved it."

Just then, the Erasers jumped onstage. Lori and Philip came over and grabbed me to go up front with them. Philip gave me a kiss as he pulled me away. I looked back at Jimmy as I left. He was staying by the bar, smoking his Parliament. There and not there.

The Erasers banged into their song "Jumped," and Philip twisted and bounced to the music. I moved away, toward the wall. I loved the Erasers. But I wasn't a dancer, a slammer, or a twister. I just loved the music. I wanted to watch and listen and think.

A few minutes later, I went to the dressing room behind the stage to get my stuff. When I turned to go back outside, Jimmy walked in and grabbed me. He didn't say a word to me; he just kissed me with a near frantic need. He didn't let me move; he held me so close and tightly. I feared he would never let go. And Philip was right outside by the stage. Just then, Lori walked in and jerked back a little. Jimmy loosened his grip and I quickly moved to a chair by the far wall. The Erasers' encore song, "I Won't Give Up," boomed from the stage as Susan screamed and took over the audience.

"Where are my cigarettes?" Lori asked, bumbling past Jimmy and diving into her bag.

A few minutes later, when the song ended, Susan and Jane came in panting with excitement and grabbed their drinks. Eraser fans streamed into the dressing room, singing and jabbering with the band. Lori and I grabbed our bags and edged out of the room. Suddenly, Lori realized she had left her leather jacket back on a chair. But by that point the place was packed with more CB's regulars and Eraser fans. I stood up on my toes to see if there was a passage we could go back through to get Lori's jacket, but I saw nothing. Suddenly my gaze froze. I saw Jimmy in there kissing Jody Beach.

Two mealy hands dragged my gut down to the floor. He was kissing Jody? I turned away and pushed past Lori.

"Hey!" she snapped. "Where are you going? We have to get my jacket outta there!"

I forced my way through the dancing and jerking CB's crowd to the front, past the bar, and through the main door into the blistering cold out front. I looked out at the night. The snow settled briskly on the street. I didn't zip my jacket. I just stood there.

Lori burst out the front door. I swung around.

"What's wrong with you?" she asked, tossing her cigarette into the snowy air.

"He kissed her."

"Who—you mean you?"

I realized that was a pretty good question.

"No one," I said.

I went back inside, got my bag, and left. It was nearly 3 a.m. The snow and the cold helped keep the streets empty. I started back home, but after I had gone about three blocks, I noticed Jimmy walking with Jody across the street. They were heading for the Erasers' loft around the corner.

I quickly crossed the street and started to follow them. I was careful to keep at least a half block distance between us. The flakes were getting bigger, assaulting my eyelids. I wiped them away.

Jimmy had his arm around Jody while they walked. After a few minutes, I saw them go to the front door of the Erasers' building. Jody opened the door and they went inside. I quickly slid up to the front and looked through the window of the door as they went up the stairs.

After they disappeared, I stepped back and just looked through that window. My heart felt lacerated. I gulped in some air. What was happening to me? I started to think about why I was there, why I had followed them. Did it matter to me that much? If that was who he wanted to be with, then that was where he should be. Then why was he relentlessly coming after me? I wondered. I stood there, snowflakes sliding down my cheeks, shaking off my tremors. Why was I here? Was this the way it is when you were an adult? Because I wasn't one of those. As much as it felt like I was, I wasn't. Why was I here? I didn't have any answers for myself. All I had was a piercing ache inside me. Was I falling in love with him?

16

CHRISTMAS WEATHER

AS WE WALKED IN MY LYMPH NODES ACHED. The amount of beige bulging everywhere was sickening. Every stick of furniture, piece of carpeting, stretch of wall in that inside world was the shade of oyster fungus, a silky, sycophantic fawn color. Everywhere: The carpets, the chairs, the couches, the receptionist's desk. All the walls were carpeted in a seedy coriander yellow. Basically, it was all the color of vomit.

I wondered if that was strategic on the part of record companies—to build the walls of their recording studios to confuse the nauseated feelings many musicians start having after being stuck in there for twenty-four to forty-eight hours straight. You had to sleep, eat, shit, and perform while creating songs and music that would sell, all while trying to hold onto your personal sense of creativity.

There were no windows anywhere—not in the waiting room or the bathrooms and certainly not the studio itself. The sense of time or space inside there was mind-numbing.

I hated it.

It was early spring in '79. After signing with Ork Records[1] we were at Blank Tape Studios, in the Flatiron district in downtown Manhattan, to

---

1 Lori says: "I don't remember getting signed by Terry Ork—maybe I'll just say, Jimmy did it.' I can remain faithful to that memory and be thankful that it happened. I do remember recording at Electric Lady Studios and I also remember a pair of orthodox Jews sitting in the control room, touching their girlfriends [*Huh?! Eww!*]. I also recall a lot of white powder sifting around, leaving its residue wherever it landed."

make a single of a few of our songs: "Christmas Weather"[2] and "Channel 13," as well as "The Quake," which Jimmy particularly liked, and which was eventually quoted in the Blondie song "Slow Motion," which I cowrote with him.

When we got there that first night—near 10 p.m.—I was exhausted. I had been up late that whole week, writing a term paper on the King Arthur legend in the Middle Ages, and it had wiped me. There was no way any of us could have done this recording during the day, given school and work. Plus, as Antone explained to me, it was cheaper to rent the studio at night. Both ends of the candle were barely flickering for all of us. Even so, we were really excited about making this single, despite the teachers and bosses and bills chomping at our heels.

The engineer who was assisting Jimmy in the control room showed us into the main waiting room. When we walked in, "The Hats" were there sitting around the table. Were they waiting for us? The Hats were a group of three Hasidic Jewish guys who were always around, it seemed. They were bearded and shadowy, settled under their black hats, endlessly smoking Salem cigarettes and eating. They represented the powers behind closed doors you never knew about and didn't want to know about. They were, I was told, the main financiers behind Terry Ork. When I sat down on the couch in the waiting room, I made sure to sit way over on the farthest end, as far away from them as possible. I looked up at the TV in the corner. Johnny Carson was shaking out Joan Rivers, and the audience was in hysterics. I looked over at the Hats. They ignored Johnny while they attacked their corned beef sandwiches, in between long drags on their Salems.

Just then, Lori plopped down next to me. She put her feet up and opened her soda.

"You okay?" she asked.

I looked over at the Hats.

"You know those guys?" I whispered to her.

"No," she said. "But Philip does."[3]

---

2   Philip remembers that we repeatedly played this song for Jimmy in rehearsals to convince him it should be on the single.

3   Philip says that around the time we were signed to Ork, he found himself doing coke in a limo with the Hats. And David recalls he was disappointed that we weren't dealing with Terry directly but with the Hats: "They were shameless drug addicts. . . . Bad, bad people."

The rest of the band had gone with Antone, to help get the equipment together in the sound room, while Lori and I sat, inconspicuously quiet, with the Hats. After a moment, I jumped up and dumped some coins in a vending machine in the corner. A ginger ale popped out at the bottom. I cracked it open and fell back on the couch. Lori got up to change the channels on the TV, settling on a rerun of *Three's Company*, and sat back down, kicking her legs back up. The Hats weren't fazed in the least. There was no one else in the room, as far as they were concerned. They just kept smoking and eating.

A little while after Chrissy slammed the door on Jack on the TV, I ventured out down the hall. Bill and Antone were moving Bill's keyboard into the sound room. I followed them in and saw a set of Ludwigs in the back. For me, I figured. I took a sip of ginger ale. Philip was sitting on his amp, tuning and playing through "Channel 13" to himself. Acoustic. Quiet. Alone.

I walked closer to him. As I did, there was a knock on the control room window. I looked up. It was Jimmy. He was waving wildly at me. I raised my soda can to him and smiled. David was with him, looking over the board and talking to the engineer. Jimmy waved for me to come in. I smiled again but turned to Philip.

"Jimmy wants us in the control room," I said to him.

The king at the controls. (PHOTO BY ANDY SCHWARTZ)

"No, he wants *you* in the control room," he said, not lifting his head while fingering his Strat.

"That's crazy," I said, sitting down next to him.

I hadn't seen Philip a lot since New Year's, except at our gigs. It didn't mean anything, except between school, watching Yancy, which I still did a little, and our shows, time was tight. Although I had started to not want to take the train out to Larchmont anymore. I was tired of that trip. I didn't want to hide in his attic bedroom. I didn't want to march endlessly through the unconscious suburban streets to the next teenage "debauchery" party. I didn't want that anymore.

When we first started dating, almost a year previously, Philip and I used to talk on the phone for hours. I would be falling asleep, near 1 a.m., and we would still be on the phone together. I remember once he was having a particularly rough time with his gym teacher at school. He didn't want to play football, he wanted to play guitar. He was constantly writing songs and playing them for me on those late-night calls. I remember him playing around with a riff that would eventually become one of our best songs. But through it all he was depressed. I saw it every time he took another swig of NyQuil, or vodka, or when he slam-danced wildly at shows of the B-52s or the Cramps. He danced with no sense of rhythm but with a tragic sense of what was missing for himself, and for all of us, really.

I watched as he played through "Christmas Weather." That was the song Jimmy wanted to record first. He had introduced some significant changes to the structure of the song, such as "bump-bumps" in the beginning and adding Bill's synthesizer intro.[4]

Philip didn't look up at me.

"Are you ready for this?" I asked him.

---

4 David recalls that Jimmy definitely "meddled with our songs." Some changes were improvements, and some, he thought, were definitely not. ("I hated the bump-bumps.") Philip said he remembers a lot of bass and drum rehearsals for the recording and that Jimmy also was responsible for the breakdown before the guitar solo in "Quake" (just like the one in Blondie's "Fan Mail"), putting the guitar line under the second verse in "Channel 13," acoustic guitar in "Looks," and maybe (probably) the "ahhhh, looks" backing vocal in that song. Philip also remembers being somewhere doing coke at 5 a.m. with a piano and playing the keyboard figure from "Samantha" to Jimmy and Bruce Brody (from the Patti Smith band) and them all jamming on that.

He didn't reply right away. Then, almost thoughtlessly, he said, "Are you?"

"No."

I turned and looked at the drums. I had to get back there, get used to them because they weren't mine. I looked around. None of this was mine, I thought, or rather, what was all this that we were doing?

Philip started playing a song I loved, the one he used to play over the phone to me as I fell asleep. I loved that song. Suddenly, Jimmy opened the sound room door.

"We have to start!" he sang through his huge smile.

"Okay," I said. I turned to Philip.

"I have to get to the drums," I said.

"Yeah."

He kept playing that song.

"Bring that in," I implored him.

"What?"

"That—that riff—that song." I said. He looked up at me and then went back to playing.

"I'm not done" he said.

"Well, when you are, bring it in."

Just then, David came over, followed by Bill and Lori. Damn, I hadn't bounced over the drums yet. I raced back there and grabbed a pair of sticks from my bag and started hitting the bass drum, the floor tom, and the snare, just to hear them. Everything sounded fine to me, although I had no great ear for the right sound. So, as usual, I merely hoped everything was good. Philip plugged into his amp and tuned up. Then he continued playing that song. No one paid attention as they got their instruments together. But I did. I heard it.

I wonder if Jimmy knew what kind of treasure was right in front of him when Philip played.

Jimmy went back into the control room. Everybody continued tuning and prepping. Jimmy had wanted to record some of our songs, almost from the moment we first met him. Even though Blondie was embarking on huge success at that time—making TV appearances and touring—Jimmy was anxious to make his mark as a producer. I think he liked our pop sound, but I think that even more he saw us as malleable. We were his midnight drink. He wanted to mix us the way it tasted best for him. He wanted to restructure our songs, our music, our lyrics and, likely, us.

After we had set up our instruments in the sound studio so Jimmy could organize the levels in the engineering room, we started playing "Christmas Weather" to get it as good as we could and to relax with it. Being behind the drums, in a walled-off studio booth, with mics everywhere and glass partitions between us to focus the sounds our instruments made, was wildly unsettling. It was a truly foreign experience, beyond much of our understanding and control.

As we blasted away on our instruments, getting focused, we jumped again into the pounding start of the song. It felt strong and together and tight. I looked at everyone and giggled. The Ludwigs felt good and instinctively easy for me. This was the way it should be. It seemed like we were really doing it.

After we finished, I threw my sticks up and we all laughed. Just then, Jimmy came in. He was applauding.

"Great, great, great!" he said. "Now we have to do it exactly like that for the recording!" he continued. "Then we need to record you individually."

Individually? How did that work?

Just then, Jimmy climbed over the world of wires and around and under the cymbals. He brushed my hair with his palm.

"You're just perfect, girl!" he exclaimed. He looked around to the rest of the guys.

"She's a perfect metronome, isn't she?"

Everybody nodded. I looked up at Jimmy. Yeah, sure, I thought, a metronome—sure. Then he put his hand on my back. The hairs on my skin shook. I looked at Philip. He turned away.

"Here," he sang, "for you." He opened a small white packet and tapped a line of cocaine onto my snare drum. I looked up at him.

"Take it!" he said, beaming. He seemed so proud and certain. He was completely at peace, though inside he was a frenzied machine in an exhilarated space, and he didn't want to be anywhere else.

I took the bill from him and sniffed up the line. He then wound his way to everyone else and they all dutifully and amiably sniffed. Jimmy leaped out and back to the control room.

"Let's do it!" he cried, waving his arms in the air.

I counted down—one, two, three—and we blasted into "Christmas Weather." I don't know if it was the cocaine, or the thrill of being in a recording studio, or the continuing rapture I felt around Jimmy since he'd become interested in us six months ago, but it seemed like we were in a dazed fantasy.

I know I was awed a little by his fast-growing fame with Blondie and stupefied by that world of rock 'n' roll stardom and celebrity clinging to the back of his belt, following him everywhere, creating him at every turn. And that only grabbed me more. Plus, we had slept together. As I carefully pounded out the beat in the studio at that moment, I looked up at Jimmy. He was looking right back at me. I turned away and kept slamming the snare, keeping the beat. I looked back at him again and he was still focused on me. And my eyes stayed there—on him.

. . .

"HI."

"Hi."

"How are you feelin'? Lori said you had a bad cold."

"Yeah."

"I'm sorry I haven't called sooner," I said.

"It's okay. It makes sense."

"What does that mean?"

"Well, you're breaking up with me."

"What? Why are you saying that?"

"Because you are. You're with Jimmy."

I didn't say anything. He coughed. I pulled the phone away. I don't know why. It was instinct. I put the phone back to my ear.

"Yeah," I said. "I guess I am."

After a short, empty moment he spoke.

"Well . . . goodbye," he said.

My heart felt like dog food.

"Yeah. I'm so sorry."

When it all began. (PHOTO BY GARY VALENTINE)

Later that afternoon I met Jimmy at his new apartment on Twentieth Street. He was very sweet and understanding, and I was feeling a little ice-covered. It was a large studio with one room down two steps and windows all around. It was on the fifteenth floor, and you could see the entire downtown when you stood in the middle of the room. There was no furniture except a double bed and a small color TV in the corner. And of course his Moog Synthesizer. I sat on the bed and Jimmy turned on the movie *Patton*. I smiled. I had seen *Patton* seven times after it was rereleased in 1974, at the local movie theater three blocks down from my mom's house in Falls Church, Virginia. I'd gone to it the day it opened and every afternoon for the next week. I don't completely know why it grabbed me but I was mesmerized by it. It may have been the intrigue of the American military, WWII, or Patton's aggressiveness. But for some reason, that movie took hold of me and I really needed to see it right then.

I jumped back on Jimmy's bed and watched as Patton marched into Sicily. Jimmy called for Chinese food and then rolled over to hold me. I could disappear now. Jimmy was holding me and, with his patience and sweetness, pulling me to him even closer. And I found myself pulling him to me.

• • •

WHEN WE FINISHED THE RECORDING AT BLANK TAPE, I learned that Jimmy was in talks with Terry Ork about the release date but it didn't sound like it would be anytime soon. I ended up moving in with him, which was a bit of a feat to pull off with my dad. But since I was in the last semester of twelfth grade, he was okay with it. However, there was a developing problem with Ms. McCray, the principal at Friends.

Somehow, Ms. McCray had gotten word I wasn't living at home, and that was not only against Friends Seminary policy, it was against the law.

On a Friday in late February, Ms. McCray pulled me out of my afternoon physics class. She took me to her office, where my dad and Jane were waiting. Great, I thought, we were in big shit. She told my dad that it was against the law for me to not be living at home and that if I didn't return right away she would revoke my scholarship to attend Friends for that last semester. She would also consider expulsion. My dad, with his peerless panache, promised Ms. McCray he would make sure I returned home and that I would be at school at the correct time every day, without fail. We rose to leave and my dad held Ms. McCray's hand for what seemed like hours, then pulled her close as he promised to respect her wishes. As we walked out, I noticed a bunch of water lilies in the vase on her desk. Dad usually gave water lilies to Jane after they had a fight.

The problem was I didn't want to move home. I wanted to stay at Jimmy's and that was my plan. I had already gone grocery shopping and made a roast chicken and mashed potatoes in the tiny kitchen for him. I was planning on my tuna salad with vinegar and apples for lunch the next day. I was the lady of that house and I wanted it to stay that way.

Turns out, Dad wanted it to stay that way as well. After that weekend, I went back to the loft and sat down with him. He was busy editing a short film he'd made based on Alfred Hitchcock's *Psycho*, in his studio in the back. I stepped in quietly. When he saw me, he pressed stop on the monitor and put down his notebook.

"So, what're we going to do?" he asked, leaning back and eyeing me.

"I don't know." I said.

"Well . . ." He stood up and walked past me. No hug, no kiss hello. I was a floor lamp. He went to the kitchen and I followed.

"You're only a few months from graduating," he continued, pouring orange juice into a small green glass. "Would be a shame to lose all that after you've done nearly four years," he said.

"Yes."

"How's the band doing?" he asked.

Sixteen going on forty-five. (PHOTO BY GARY VALENTINE)

"Good," I replied. "The single should be out soon."

"Right," he remarked.

He walked back to his studio. I followed, again. He sat back in his chair and picked up his pen and notebook and looked up at the monitor.

"I'm at school every day, Dad," I said.

"Not on time," he replied.

He leaned toward the video monitor and was about to press the play button but turned to me.

"Get there on time, every day," he said emphatically, with little thought about it all. "I don't want to hear from McCray again."

Then he pressed play.

MB: She was
there with me
through it all.
(PHOTO BY
DANA KINSTLER)

Bill capturing
me in hysterics
when I was in
ninth grade!
(PHOTO BY
BILL ARNING)

The Mumps.
Live, irresistible
rock 'n' roll chaos.
(© JENNY LENS)

CBGB: Can't count the number of hours
I lived in here, we all lived in here.
(PHOTO BY DAVID GODLIS)

Best Girls:
The doorkeeper
to the kingdom
and the rising star.
(PHOTO BY
BOBBY GROSSMAN)

The sweetest
bouncer in
the world.
(PHOTO BY
DAVID GODLIS)

First poster!
(PHOTO BY MICHAEL ALAGO; POSTER DESIGNED BY BILL ARNING)

Student Teachers photo session.
(PHOTO BY STEVE LOMBARDI)

Lori and me at the Hot Club.
(PHOTO BY STEVE LOMBARDI)

Trying to keep up.
(PHOTO BY
STEVE LOMBARDI)

Jane, me, Lori,
and Jody
plotting world
domination.
(PHOTO BY
JOE STEVENS)

Working it! (PHOTO BY STEVE LOMBARDI)

Live at
CBGB, 1979.
(PHOTO BY
DAVID GODLIS)

Bill live at
CBGB, 1979.
(PHOTO BY
DAVID GODLIS)

17

CONTRAVENTION

IN LATE FEBRUARY '79, JIMMY AND BLONDIE were filming music videos for "Heart of Glass" and other songs promoting their *Parallel Lines* album. The filming was being done at SIR studios on Fifty-Second Street.

The first thing that hit me when I walked in was how unearthly the place was and it made me wildly nervous. The room was a football field. There were roadies and techies and makeup people, costume people, photographers—and then, in the middle of the soundstage, the rest of the guys in the band huddled around their instruments, laughing and eating whatever food floated past them. They tuned and played bits in chord sequences and songs as Jimmy sauntered over. I hung behind.

"Hey, assholes!" he shouted.

They threw their food at him. I moved to a table in the corner and sat down.

After a few minutes of tweaking and banging out practice pieces of "Heart of Glass," Debbie joined them. The director then went over to get them all going. Debbie walked into the center of the soundstage and hovered by the mic. She spoke to the guys for a sec, then they broke into "Heart of Glass"—the star of the moment.

It was thrilling to be there—earsplitting and overwhelming. Cameramen moved around the band and the director wandered in front, his hand on his chin, contemplating. Although I felt a little fraudulent as I sat there watching them, that was not a surprising feeling to have while sitting inside the world of big-time rock 'n' roll. They were the darlings of the moment, the shooting stars of the music world, and the most prevalent feeling that I experienced was that of a tagalong. Unfortunately, that feeling never went away. It was at every concert, on every tour. That was the role of the rock 'n' roll girlfriend—to be quiet, attentive, and, most of all, a ghost.

As Debbie sang, her voice and her elegance enveloped the entire space. The band was so much fun to watch and Clem Burke, particularly, was practically jumping out of his seat behind the drums—he was having such a blast.

This was worlds away from the little rehearsals in my drum teacher's loft or the small studios we rehearsed in around the city, realms away from the downtown scene of cramped nighttime gigs. Although everyone started somewhere, this felt, as I took it all in, so very far from where I was or even where I might end up.

After the first run-through, Jimmy came over and gave me a kiss and a bottle of Pepsi. The other guys ambled up behind him.

"This is Clem," Jimmy said, pointing at the dark, muscular drummer as he approached. His hair was impeccably styled and he seemed a little self-conscious but lovable.

"Ignore him," Jimmy remarked. Clem kicked him, laughing.

I waved to Nigel as he came over. Even though I had met him before, at Horatio Street, I wasn't sure if he remembered me. I knew he was new to the band. He wore tight black pants and a beautiful tailored striped shirt. I learned later that his focus was his fashion and that he was always perfectly outfitted. Jimmy then introduced me to Frank Infante, who had joined the band when Gary left. He seemed very different, not like a carefully coiffed pop musician, but more distant and grungier and as sweet as the other guys, if not more so. I smiled at him.

"Hey, I'm Chris." That was Debbie's boyfriend, Chris Stein. I knew him from the albums.

"So, why are you here?" he coyly asked, strumming his guitar as he wandered around me.

Jimmy jumped in.

"This is Laura. She's the drummer for the Student Teachers. I'm producing their single."

"Oh, you are?" Chris sang. "Interesting," he continued, letting his eyes drift all over me. He zigzagged away, madly fingering his guitar.

Debbie was huddled in the far corner with someone doing her makeup as she talked to the director. Although she was far back in the corner of the room, as I watched her, she radiated. She stood out above everyone else. She was alone in that shining light, though. She exuded a kind of

It was all on her. (PHOTO BY CHRIS STEIN)

solitariness—a needed space, needed "alone" air. And I don't think it was just because of her looks.

Although I didn't meet her at that session, I eventually did talk with her. She was engaging and soft-spoken but definitely existed a few steps away. Despite the fact that she was always serious and focused when I was around her, I know she had fun sometimes. I remember once when we were in Dallas during a short U.S. tour, she was visited backstage by an old girlfriend from high school who'd just had a baby, and Debbie's girliness and sweetness gushed out everywhere.

But there was never a sit-down with her behind a stage or at a bar or a diner, like with the rest of the band. She was always a distance away. I think the fame Blondie was carrying at that moment wasn't a shock to her—she had been in the music business for a long time—she was nine years older than Jimmy. But the level of the fame, the sudden meteoric rise, was overwhelming. And most of it rested on her.

After the tapings, Jimmy and the rest of the band—except Debbie and Chris—always went out on the town. It was usually to dinner at a restaurant in the theater district because the soundstage was near there, and, afterward, to a nightclub. One evening, when some of the filming had finished, Jimmy hired a limo and everyone climbed in to go to Studio 54. It seemed strange to me to have a limo take us only a few blocks away but Jimmy didn't care about the distance—it was the impression he wanted to make when we arrived.

That was very Jimmy. He was seriously concerned with the impression of a given idea, or event, or action. He didn't always take the time to look at what was behind the makeup or the craft or the words. He wanted to do whatever would help him achieve his goal. It didn't matter that it was made of smoke and mirrors.

• • •

I REGULARLY MADE MY FAVORITE TUNA FISH SALAD and hard-boiled eggs at Twentieth Street. I kept the bathroom spotless and did the laundry at the Laundromat around the corner. I also started to help with the Blondie fan club, which was being run by Roberta Bayley. She was working as a photographer, but because she was a good friend of Debbie's, she helped oversee the fan club, and I joined her. Every Wednesday, after school ended, I took the subway to the post office at Third Avenue and Fifty-Fourth Street, where the Blondie fan club had their post office box, and lugged the bag of accumulated mail back to Twentieth Street.

The goal was to answer as many letters as possible. A lot of them were from very young fans—twelve-, thirteen-year-olds. Some were from mothers and fathers writing about their sick child who just wanted to hug Debbie. It was heart-wrenching to reply to those letters but I had to do it. I remember sitting at our small dining table sifting through the bag, hoping to get as much done as possible, but the amount of letters filled a huge duffel bag. Between homework and the letters, I was hard-pressed.

One Wednesday afternoon, Jimmy came home from rehearsal and told me he was off to Europe the following week on the Concorde. He was so excited. He immediately ran into the bathroom and threw cold water on his face. Maybe he was trying to make sure it was all real, that all the unbelievable success he was suddenly living through was genuine, I don't know.

"God! I wish I could take you with me!" he said, grabbing me and carrying me to the bed.

"I begged Terry Ellis at Chrysalis to let you come with me but he said it was too expensive." He pulled off his shirt and then pulled off mine. "Will you be okay here, by yourself?"

"Of course," I said. "Don't worry about it."

He pulled off my jeans and started tickling me.

"Jimmy!" I screamed, laughing harder than I could breathe. He covered me with kisses. Then suddenly the doorbell rang.

"Damn!" Jimmy pulled back and picked up his pants.

"Who is it?" he screamed.

I quickly put my clothes on.

"It's Chris!" someone yelled. "Open the door!"

Jimmy lit up a cigarette and raced to the door.

"Hey!" he said and pulled Chris into the living room. He was all smiles. "This is Laura. She's a drummer just like you, Chris."

I stood up and waved.

"Laura, this is Chris Frantz." I recognized him of course, from Talking Heads, but I didn't want to make too much of it. I had to be cool. I dashed around the place, picking up the mess. Jimmy pulled Chris to the dining room table and asked me to call for some Chinese food. Then he broke open a packet of coke onto the table as he jousted with Chris about both of their next albums. He was gone now, far away from me.

18

CANNOLI

SINCE JIMMY WAS LEAVING AT THE BEGINNING of the following week, he decided we should go to Staten Island. It was time to meet the parents.

Jimmy had been born in Brooklyn, and although his parents lived there for most of his life, they had recently moved to Staten Island. Jimmy came from a strong and loyal Italian family with a long history in Brooklyn and a hot-blooded commitment to all their relatives.

Every Sunday was family day, and though Jimmy usually missed the dinners due to his schedule, he tried to make it to some of them. He adored his mother, and every Sunday she cooked a feast of Italian specialties that could easily have fed a sold-out crowd at Yankee Stadium.

I was thrown into pure culture shock when I was first driven out to meet his family. It wasn't as if I hadn't been to Staten Island before, but when I had, it was just briefly. Not far off from the Verrazano-Narrows Bridge, which connected Staten Island to Brooklyn, Jimmy's parents lived in a newly built family housing complex. It was located right in front of Willowbrook State School, which I was told about when we arrived there. I eyed that place carefully. It looked very old and melancholy, and was famous for housing mentally ill children. It looked straight out of a black-and-white movie from the '30s and existed in a different dimension. As Jimmy's mom came up and gave me a big, loving hug, I was sure that hospital right behind her was somewhere else. It didn't make any sense.

Right through the front door of his parents' house was the dining room, and the kitchen was in the back. The aromas of succulent Italian sausage and pasta greeted me the moment I walked in. It was amazing.

I came from a very distant life in SoHo, where people worked seven days a week. My family didn't have family dinner days. Jane was a writer more than a cook, and her signature dish, beef bourguignon (she was a Francophile), did not sit well with the teenage palate. I came from stringent, white-walled artist lofts, whereas Jimmy was from close-knit, warmly thawed rooms covered in family photos and overflowing with yummy hot Italian peppers.

At the huge feast of pasta with meatballs, ravioli, cannelloni, and Italian breads, Jimmy talked breathlessly about taking the Concorde to Europe and Blondie's promotional tour there the following week. He was easily the star of the family, and his parents didn't hide it. Even though his sister, Donna Destri, a stunning Elizabeth Taylor look-alike, was starting to take the New York rock scene by storm with her own band, her sensual singing, and unmistakable style, Jimmy was the king. And though his parents seemed to have an uneasiness with me—I was closer in age to Jimmy's fifteen-year-old brother—it didn't matter much.

After dinner, his parents hung around the table to talk and enjoy coffee, cigarettes, cannoli, and, sometimes, a card game. On this occasion, Jimmy went outside and sat on the front steps to smoke and wait for his cousin, who was coming by to see the resident rock star. I watched him go out the front door, promising he'd be back in a minute, while I sat there with his parents, alone.

"How about some cannoli, honey?" his mother offered. "James gets them from Veniero's in the city every Friday."

"Thank you," I said, "but I'm stuffed." I smiled as genuinely as I could.

"No, no, no!" she said as she raced to the kitchen and opened the big white box on the counter.

"We got these especially for Jimmy!" she said. "He loves his Sunday cannoli!" and she brought me a plate. I smiled and nodded, though the only thought I had was, *But I'm not Jimmy.*

Food was everything to Jimmy's family. That was such a different universe from mine in downtown Manhattan. On the rare weekend when my father and Jane went out of town on business, they usually left us some milk, Sugar Pops cereal, a can of escarole soup, and nothing else.

Food was but a minor source of fuel for us. For Jimmy's family, it was the meaning of life.

A few minutes later, Jimmy barreled back in with his cousin in tow. They wanted to go for a drive in the old Brooklyn neighborhood. There was a lot of howling, bantering, and razzing between them as they got themselves together. Jimmy gave his mom and dad a big bear hug and slipped his younger brother a twenty.

"Donna!" he screamed. "Come with us!"

Everyone climbed into Jimmy's cousin's Toyota. I sat on Jimmy's lap as we raced through the Staten Island streets to the Verrazano Bridge. It was near midnight and the ocean air from under the bridge gushed in through the open windows. It felt brisk and intoxicating. I hadn't said a word since we left. It was family time in the Bay Ridge–bound car.

The night lasted till three, and they drove around, looking at where Jimmy and Donna had grown up and gone to school. They were all missing their childhoods, but Jimmy particularly. I remember watching his sadness crescendo as we cruised past the house he grew up in and the school he went to as a brash young teen. Though every time he had the chance, he screamed out of the open car window:

"Hey, world! Didn't go to college and I'm richer than you bastards!"

He bellowed his bravado, which was endearing at first and fired up by his family's exuberant pride for him, but what I saw was something very different. More often than not, there was deep pain in his eyes. Maybe that's what drew me to him, because I always had an obsessive need— itself psychologically destructive—to take care of everyone, and I could see in him a murkier, sadder reality that he hid away as much as possible. I knew he wanted to feel better about himself, but as he climbed out of the Toyota onto the playground of his old school and took out a packet of coke with his cousin—my heart sank.

• • •

WHILE JIMMY WAS AWAY IN EUROPE and then on a short U.S. tour after that, which included playing on *The Midnight Special* and *American Bandstand*, the Student Teachers continued performing every weekend. Before he left, Jimmy had gotten in touch with Jerry Nolan, the drummer for the New York Dolls and, at that time, the Heartbreakers. Jerry was selling his pink drums. We suspected he needed the money to fuel his heroin habit, but Jimmy thought that they would be a great set for me—maybe because I was a girl, though that didn't make sense. I never wore pink. Nothing I owned was pink. I wasn't pink. But for the drums, pink worked really well.

Jimmy and Jerry had been friends for a while, and though I understood it was largely under the garland of drugs, they got along well and the drums were great. How cool. How eye-catching, except I don't remember seeing Jerry at all after we bought the drums.

Jimmy flew off on the Concorde and I continued to dig in as much as possible to make sure I graduated from Friends on June 15.

Making my 8:30 a.m. gym class was a continual struggle. I was consistently late and I couldn't understand why anyone wanted to be in, or even semiconscious for, a gym class at that time in the morning. I tried the best I could. Even worse, I wasn't cutting it in Mr. Schwartz's class on King Arthur and the British world of 1150, which met right after gym.

"Ms. Davis!" I jumped.

I wasn't asleep, but I was nearly there.

"Yes, sir," I dutifully replied.

"Tell me about *Vita Merlini*, Ms. Davis." He tapped my shoulder with his knuckle. My eyes lifted up to him and his flashing colors of annoyance.

"That was a book written about the life of Merlin," I said, squeezing my brain synapses to remember more.

"Yes, we know that. What does it say about him?"

"Uh . . . that he was a madman."

Mr. Schwartz wandered around the room.

"Who wrote it, Ms. Davis?"

Good question.

"It wasn't Arthur, obviously," I murmured, my nose crinkling.

"Obviously!" he said. "Speak up!"

"Was it autobiographical?" I offered, hoping, like the king's fool in front of the uninterested monarch, to start up a dialogue.

Just then, the period bell rang and everyone gathered their books and ran out. I threw my textbook into my bag and turned to get out of my chair, but I was immediately stopped by the presence of Mr. Schwartz, who loomed over me. I gazed upward.

"Sir?"

The room emptied. I stayed seated. Mr. Schwartz went to the front and didn't look back at me.

"Why aren't you doing better?"

I looked down at my knees.

"You're earning a C+," he said.

I nodded. He turned around and looked at me sternly.

"Are you planning to improve that grade?"

"Yes, sir," I said.

"If you don't, you risk not graduating," he warned. I knew that. I knew that very well.

When school finished that afternoon, I walked back to Twentieth Street like I did every day. I was very tired, as much from the gigs and the rehearsals as I was from the taxing schoolwork. And living with Jimmy too. It felt like something had to give, that I couldn't do this—keep playing gigs and make it through to graduation.

But, as I did with a lot of reflective thoughts then, I pushed my worries aside. I always had this weird feeling that if I thought of an action, or an event, or an answer to a question, it would happen—or it wouldn't. For instance, I was always very careful not to think about getting an A on an exam, because then it wouldn't happen. Somehow, I had this sense, far deep inside me, that if I really wanted something to happen, it wouldn't, and that if I really didn't want something to happen, it would. Once, when I was walking home from the deli around the corner from the apartment, I saw a woman being pushed in a wheelchair. She wasn't an older woman, or a senior; she was nearer my age, maybe twenty-five. She had long blonde hair and seemed very petite. She was talking to the man pushing her chair. Maybe it was her husband. Maybe not. I remember thinking how awful it would be to live like that, not being able to walk.

PART 2

19

MARS

IT WAS IN THE LATE SUMMER OF 1979 when I met him. Jimmy and I were in a cab going uptown to Debbie and Chris's house near Central Park for one of their impromptu get-togethers when he told me.

"So, Bowie's going to be there, you know."

My lungs suddenly stiffened. I looked over at him.

"What?" I spluttered.

I gasped quickly to get back to breathing.

"Yeah," Jimmy said. "He's doing some work with Debbie, so he's going to be there." He fished for his Parliaments and opened the cab window as he lit up. I stared out my side, recovering from the loss of oxygen, watching the city's buildings scale past me, then disappear. I thought about seeing him at the Garden with Bill a few years back—how far away he'd been on that stage—explosive and spiraling into the ether above us. I thought about the *Aladdin* album, and *Ziggy Stardust. Ziggy Stardust. Ziggy.*

"Stop that," Jimmy said when the cab driver hit the brakes at Fifty-Eighth Street.

"Stop what?" I asked.

Did he know what I was thinking? Maybe when I got upstairs, they would all know. Maybe they all knew that I was just a starstruck teenager who believed that Bowie was Ziggy, that he had come down from Mars and that I was his contact on earth, that I was here to save him, that I was not one of them, that I was not a rock musician or anywhere near it, that I was a fraud and that I shouldn't be there.

A more than perfect match. (PHOTO BY CHRIS STEIN)

When we stopped at the curb in front of their building and jumped out of the cab, Jimmy grabbed me and kissed me.

"Stop looking so beautiful," he said, pulling me closer.

I squeaked out a jutting sigh as he let go and headed to the front door. I shook myself and wobbled behind him.

The best thing about Debbie and Chris's apartment was that it had a huge kitchen, and the floor was covered in cool black and white tiles. I have a distinct memory of that kitchen floor, because whenever we visited, I spent most of my time in there. It's not that the rest of the place wasn't great—they lived in a one-bedroom penthouse with a sweeping balcony outside that looked onto the entire West Side of the city. The place wasn't huge but it was warm and charming. Because the front door opened onto the kitchen, I always took the opportunity to hang back and just linger there, slipping my mind into the black and white tiles.

That night, when we entered, the place was streaming with people. Jimmy dashed through the kitchen to the living room and I, well . . . I stood in the doorway. All the Blondies were there and a bunch of people I didn't know, hanging around, talking and drinking.

"Hi, honey, you want a drink? We have everything," Debbie said to me as she brushed by and tapped my forehead.

"No, thanks," I said and watched her get a bottle of wine and a plate of little cheeses out of the fridge. When the stage lights went off and the curtains closed, Debbie, the true hostess, emerged.

I couldn't really see into the entire living room because there were so many people standing around. After Debbie went back in, though, and the group shuffled and parted, that's when I saw him. He was sitting at the end of the sofa feverishly talking to Jimmy. My entire self clenched with disbelief.

He had short, vibrant chestnut-blonde hair with a carefully styled tuft that kept falling over his eyes and that he pushed back from time to time. He was wearing a black business shirt with a jacket and dark slacks, drinking a glass of white wine and laughing. Even from my distance, I could see that his skin was pale and iridescent—tanzanite—untouchable, under glass. His smile was so wide and all-encompassing—infectious and blinding—and his deep blue eyes exploded every time he smiled, which he did a lot. He was remarkably at ease. His body moved without any effort. His joints were pure water—clear, smooth, flawless. He leaned back into the sofa, smiling and comfortable with himself. He reached his arm around the back of the couch and stretched his chest a little. I silently gasped. He was heart-stoppingly beautiful.

A few people sat around him and Jimmy, but not everyone in the room. Why was that? Why wasn't everyone in that apartment sitting silently around him, kneeling before him in reverence? I snuck around the corner of the doorjamb and swiftly slipped onto an ottoman. I took a glass of wine from the table next to it. I felt so comfortable getting down low, hoping, praying no one noticed me—always seeking to hide.

Luckily Nigel ambled over and, within moments, sat next to me, so I was hidden from the crowd, and from Bowie, encapsulating my towering fear.

"Hey!"

"Hey, how are you?" I said.

"Bowie's here, you see?"

"Yeah," I said, as unemotionally as possible. "How's the recording coming?" I continued, quietly sipping my wine. I was keeping it together—cool, dispassionate.

"Laura!" Jimmy suddenly screamed from across the room.

I jumped and jerked my head up. Damn! So much for my attempt to disappear. I looked briefly at Nigel, who just giggled. I slowly stood up. Slowly and carefully, tiptoeing on sharp grains of fear, I went over to Jimmy.

"Honey, this is David!" he said fiercely, blowing smoke out of his lips as he smiled. He was ringing with excitement. I desperately hoped, tried to convert myself into someone else, somewhere else, into a role, a character—Meryl Streep, perhaps. I reached my hand out and broadly bared my teeth.

"Nice to meet you," I said, and touched his hand, feeling my heart ripping through my rib cage. "I'm a big fan."

What a stupid thing to say! I immediately thought. Who in this world is not a big fan of his?

"Good to meet you too," he said as he shook my hand, which I knew I would never wash again, or wipe again, or touch again, or rub again. That hand was now the fodder of the gods.

It was hard to speak when I was near him. (PHOTO BY EBET ROBERTS)

"This is Coco," he continued, putting his arm around the woman next to him. She was a petite, lovely looking woman with dark brown hair and an attractive but stern face. I learned later that she was his "handler"—Corinne Schwab—essentially, his everything. I reached over and shook her hand.

A moment later, Chris called us into the next room to hear a new song he was recording. Jimmy and David hurried in, throwing their arms around each other as they launched into industry talk. Hesitantly, I followed behind but lingered by the door. I needed to recover, to reconstruct my place in this new reality—from that of a fan, an onlooker, a distant scream in the back of the stadium—to something so far beyond my wildest dreams. I was having trouble finding that place.

20

SPIKES

GRADUATING FROM FRIENDS ENDED UP BEING a very thorny experience. Though I tried to make up for my constant lateness and for missing so many early morning gym and art classes, Ms. McCray couldn't find a compromise to allow me to earn my diploma that June. Even after my dad worked his magic on her, it became clear she had had enough.

Despite the school not technically graduating me, she did allow me to participate in the ceremony. I would just not be called up to accept a diploma. Although this felt to me like a pyrrhic victory of sorts, and though a large part of me didn't want to go, my dad insisted.

By that time, Jimmy and I had moved into a small duplex with a loft bedroom upstairs on Jones Street, in Greenwich Village. MB was over a lot, and we ended up shopping for my graduation dress at Macy's together, then bringing it back to the apartment, where I put it on and tried to feel, well, normal. We also picked up some pink high heels with white bows on the front. I absolutely hated them but MB thought it was better to wear them than my signature black flats. She was probably right. Even though she was a year younger than me, of the two of us, she was way older. Jimmy was really encouraging as well. They both said I should do this: appear at graduation despite the school and Ms. McCray's intolerant diminishment of me.

Jimmy wanted to pick me up in a limousine after graduation ended but I didn't let him. He was always antagonistic toward authority and institutions of all kinds, especially school. Maybe because he'd barely graduated high school himself but had achieved success despite not taking the traditional road—I don't know. But he relished any opportunity to stick it to the big guy.

I attended graduation and the brief reception afterward, with my dad, Jane, and MB. They were very pleased about it all, though the only reason I attended the reception was to find Mr. Schwartz. I hadn't seen him during the ceremony, and I wanted to say goodbye. I rushed around the school and finally found him outside of the front door, saying goodbye to some other students. I ran over to him.

"Mr. Schwartz!"

He turned to me with a bit of surprise.

"Well, Ms. Davis. You attended after all."

"Yes, I did."

He picked up his briefcase. It ballooned out. He was taking a lot of papers and work home for the summer. He started to walk down the front steps and toward the corner. He didn't invite me to join him. But I did.

"Are you off for the summer sir?"

"No, no," he said. "I'm going to England to do some research at Oxford."

"Oh," I said. "On what?"

I stumbled. My graduation gown kept getting caught under my heels. I tried not to fall. God, I hated high heels. I'd never worn them before and haven't worn them since, convinced the entire concept was created by some sadist bent on ruining women's feet.

When Mr. Schwartz reached the corner, I quickly limped up behind him. He turned to me.

"Ms. Davis, that's not what your concern should be."

"Sir?" I asked.

"You're not leaving here with a diploma, Ms. Davis."

"Yes, sir, but—"

"Are you still in that band?" he asked harshly.

"Yes," I said, though I didn't feel as proud as I'd thought I would—or should.

"Are you thinking about college?" he asked with a sharp look into my eyes. He knew this mattered.

"Not right now," I said. "I have to take a course this summer to get my diploma first."

"Yes, you do," he said.

The streetlight turned green. He looked over at me.

"Think about your choices, Ms. Davis," he said, stepping off the curb. "You can do more. Much more," he said.

"More than what?" I asked.

"Than what you're doing now," he replied. He waved at me as he started across the street. "Goodbye."

"Goodbye," I said, and waved back to him. "I'll miss you," I whispered, quieter than the shadows lurking behind me.

Though there had been a lot of noise about a "graduation party to end all parties" being held across town later that night, I decided not to attend. It had been so long since I felt a part of Friends, it seemed just too strange for me to think of joining a celebration for something I wasn't a part of and, honestly, didn't deserve.

I went back to the apartment with my sister, where Jimmy was working on a recording with his friends in a makeshift recording studio he had set up in the living room. He was working on his keyboard with a tune he thought he and I could write the lyrics for, but I was really beaten down. The goodbye with Mr. Schwartz had upset me more than I wanted to admit.

I sat down at the dining room table, kicked off my stupid high heels, and attacked the roast beef hero MB and I had picked up at the deli.

Jimmy kept playing music and started humming a tune. I glanced at him. It was a good melody. I started humming along with him. Rhyming words wove into my head like they did for him.

She can put you up on a shelf until she wants to pull the string
Still you know she'll never slip away
Keep time in your head, counting in your head[1]

---

1   "Slow Motion" by Jimmy Destri and Laura Davis from Blondie's *Eat to the Beat*, 1979.

But I still wasn't there. I was back outside Friends, sneaking up behind Mr. Schwartz. Why, I didn't know. Was it him or his words or . . . what he represented to me?

Later, to celebrate my graduation, Jimmy took a bunch of us to the Mudd Club, where we ran into Nigel and Browner and a collection of other people. It was another endless night of loud music, drugs, and lost conversations. Eventually, the group moved to an after-hours club near St. Marks Place. There was a pinball machine and a pool table. It was fun dancing and drinking and playing with my friends, and of course it turned into a coke-infused night, with Jimmy at the helm.

We left the club at 6 a.m., as the sun was rising above the Empire State Building, stringing itself around the needle at the top, announcing the workday morning. As we hailed a cab to go home, I saw business suits racing to their offices, briefcases dancing beside them. It hit me hard at that moment that leaving the clubs at early dawn was happening way too much in my life.

• ● •

DURING THE SUMMER OF '79, we played an even more hectic slate of shows. The single we had recorded with Jimmy at Blank Tape Studios a few months earlier was set to be released in the fall. Luckily, I only had to take one course at the New School for Social Research, a university only a few blocks away from Friends, to get the number of credits required for my diploma, and I only needed to be there one evening every week. I could easily keep up with the gig schedule.

We did shows with new and established acts like the Speedies, Wayne County, and the Fleshtones. And, then, for one gig, we opened for John Cale, an icon on the music scene from his days in the Velvet Underground, which was thrilling for us. We also opened for Richard Lloyd, an original member of Television, and for Donna Destri, Jimmy's sister. We were pushing ourselves as much as possible.

In early July, the Bloodless Pharaohs opened for us. They were fronted by Brian Setzer, who went on to fame with the Stray Cats and the Brian Setzer Orchestra. Curiously, he was a friend of Ellen's, our resident go-go dancer, because her brother, Ken Kinnally, was the keyboard player for the Bloodless Pharaohs.

At one gig, when we were opening for the Erasers at CB's, we took a foolish and heart-pounding trip out to Long Island after our sound check. Our plan was to see the Bloodless Pharaohs rehearse before we had to get back to the city and go onstage. The whole trip was a shrieking close call for all of us, as David, who was at the wheel of the car, dodged Saturday traffic. And we couldn't find the rehearsal studio. We kept squeezing our hands together because we were losing against the clock. We had to get back for the show at CB's. On top of that, we had some of the Erasers' equipment in the trunk of our car. Maybe we just wanted to live inside the risk. It just seemed stupid to me—to all of us. But we got there and wound up seeing the amazingly talented Brian Setzer singing backup on "Hotwire My Heart." We all knew he was a star already, long before the Stray Cats. And, luckily, we made it back to our own show, though by a hair.

. • .

JIMMY, MEANWHILE, WAS ON A U.S. TOUR with Blondie, so I was on my own at the Jones Street apartment.

There was an unspoken reality in the world of rock 'n' roll relationships when one person was on tour and the other person was at home. And that reality involved fidelity. Rock 'n' roll relationships often incorporated a different version of loyalty. The concept of fidelity becomes a bewildering, often hurtful roller-coaster ride. Of course, I was aware of this, but I think I believed that, without question, when two people made a commitment to one another, that was to be valued. Unfortunately, I learned that, in the course of his numerous trips out of town, for Jimmy, "value" took on a different meaning.

When we lived at Jones Street, we often spent late nights at one of Jimmy's friends' houses, and this friend's specialty was procuring cocaine. People like him survived by dealing, and they made a pretty good living at it, too. Their homes became a kind of bus station for customers. Often there were pool tables where people hung out, did drugs, and played pool. Or there might be a regular poker or gin rummy game happening. People just dropped in, bought drugs, then stuck around while getting high and hacking into whatever entertainment was on the table that night. It's not that I wasn't part of this whole group—it was a way of life for Jimmy and me and a lot of people we knew. It was rock 'n' roll, it was money, it was the rich man's way to get high in a private place and support whoever the dealer was of the moment—and people had fun. They loved the mystery of it all, the clandestine world. And they loved the drugs. Especially Jimmy.

One of Jimmy's friends lived around the corner from our apartment, and his name was Eddie. His place was open to everyone, at all hours. A bunch of us would go there and hang out, get high on cocaine, and play poker late into the night. Eddie wasn't particularly handsome, but he was young, energetic like Jimmy, and, by that time, rich, so there were a lot of beautiful girls around. I don't remember talking to many of them, although in fleeting moments they seemed nice. I didn't really want to associate with them. I believed I was better than that.

But I really wasn't.

One girl, I distinctly remember. She was my height and had short light brown hair, with a tomboy charm about her. As I understood it, she was Eddie's girlfriend. Her name was Jess, and she was there every time we popped by. I didn't talk to her much, but Jimmy did. I didn't make much of it because I was usually with MB and our other girlfriends—we were busy talking and giggling while everyone else wandered about getting high. I didn't make much of it when I started noticing Jess showing up at Student Teacher shows, either. She was a fan, I figured. Of course, I learned later she was more than a fan.

I don't know how it happened, but somehow she ended up at Blondie shows when they were on their U.S. tour that summer, and she and Jimmy had a long affair out of town. I'm not sure how I figured it out, but I believe Eddie told me some curious things and then I put two and two together. I felt like a piece of fermented human garbage, not quite ready for the sanitation truck to pick up, but left on the curb to stink in the heat.

I didn't know what to do.

When Jimmy got back from the tour, I confronted him about it. He didn't deny it and he apologized endlessly, swearing his love and devotion. Then he took a hit of coke. Then another. Then another.

"Let's work on that song again. Come on, honey!" he begged as he pulled me from the table where I was trying to eat some Cheerios. But I didn't want to. I needed to breathe. I needed to think.

"Come on!" he insisted, pulling me harder away from my chair.

"Jimmy!" I yanked away from him. "I need to think."

"What the fuck is there to think about? It was nothing. Nothing! And I won't do it again!"

I didn't believe him. I moved back to my chair and sat down. I took a bite of cereal.

"Laura! Get over it! I'm here, with you! I love you, dammit!" he screamed, starting to retch.

My head turned. I looked at him.

"I can't take this!" he howled, and kicked the sofa.

I watched the skin on his face start to turn sharp red. He kicked the chairs, then the table.

"What's going on?" I asked him. Something was different. He started throwing papers and books. His eyes were vibrating, his head was shaking. He quickly poured out some coke on the table and sniffed it.

I dropped my spoon and stood up.

"Maybe you should cool off on that," I said.

"Don't tell me what to do! And you gotta believe me! I love you!"

I tried to take his hand. I started getting scared.

"Okay, okay. Relax, okay?" I told him.

I tried to get hold of him but he swiped me away. He swung around and suddenly lost his balance, then fell over and slammed—face-first—into the brick wall on the side of the apartment. He slumped to the floor. I quickly ran to him.

"Jimmy! Jimmy!" I screamed. I got a wet wash cloth from the kitchen and put it on his face.

"Are you okay? Say something!" I begged.

Blood streamed down the side of his head. He groaned.

"What happened?" he mumbled.

"You fell down," I said. I helped him get to his feet.

He began shaking. His teeth chattered. I helped him upstairs and into bed. I covered him with as many blankets as I could find, then turned on the TV and sat in bed next to him. After a few moments, his hand snuck up out of the covers over to mine. He opened his fist, and in it was a box. I took it and opened it. There was a small diamond ring shining up at me. Through cracked, swollen eyes, he looked up. Tiny tears fell onto the sheet.

I saw it starting to happen to him. (PHOTO BY BILL ARNING)

"Marry me?" he asked, through broken gasps.

I looked at the ring.

Then at him.

I smiled.

And so did he. Then his head slid back and he fell asleep.

This was the beginning of the cumulative effect that cocaine was having on him. I suspected that then, and I know it now. I could see it in the person he was and the one he was turning into. The cocaine was starting to enslave him and change the way his brain worked.

21

INTEMPERANCE

AFTER I FINISHED MY COURSE IN AMERICAN LIT at the New School and my diploma was forwarded to my dad, I found I was a little lost. I still thought of myself as the drummer for the Student Teachers, although my hold on that was slipping. Not in actuality, but in my mind, in my heart. I think I was living in some kind internal disarray. It wasn't just that I didn't know where I was—I did feel a little clueless—but that I wasn't comfortable with it. Except I hadn't figured that out yet.

I bounced between clubs, staying until the morning sun broke, then sleeping all day. Jimmy didn't have a problem with this schedule. He adored the midnight hours—in fact, he relished them. He used them when we got home from a club, or even if we didn't go out, to record and write. He was a machine. He never stopped. Almost every night, when I went to bed, he said he would be upstairs in a little while, but then I'd find him still awake the next morning as I stepped down the stairs—in the same position at his synthesizer. Happened all the time.

A sudden and unique fissure in the fabric of our daily life popped up, in early fall, when Jimmy said that Bowie had called him and wanted to get together for dinner. He also told Jimmy to bring me along. I couldn't believe it. Even more frightening, I was going to have to find a way to talk to Bowie, not only in an "adult" way, but in an interesting and intelligent way. I was completely beyond myself. How in the world would I handle this?

His truest love. (PHOTO BY LISA JANE PERSKY)

That night, we took a cab to Frankie and Johnnie's Steakhouse, in the theater district. When we got out of the cab, I looked around. "Frankie and Johnnie's . . ." Where . . . where? I couldn't find the place. Small drops of rain started to float down.

Jimmy said he was sure he had the right address—West Thirty-Seventh Street—but we still couldn't find it. That restaurant was deeply veiled somehow, and for good reason, I thought. This first confused and mysterious step nearing a big mainstream legend like Bowie made me realize the weight and complications that come with being close to that kind of fame.

Finally, we found a small awning with the name on it and a dank, gray, uninviting door. When we opened it, there were stairs leading up to another bleak, nondescript door. When we opened that one, though, a luxurious gold-trimmed dining room with buttery linen tablecloths and flames burning in a fireplace against the back wall exploded in front of us. It was startling.

The place was full of people who didn't turn at the sound of the door opening, or waiters walking around—at anything. There seemed to be a distinct and unspoken directive that when you entered this restaurant, you were to be discreet and not bother anyone. We looked around. No Bowie.

A moment later, an older gentleman approached us and asked who we were and why we were there. Why? To have dinner, idiot. It was a restaurant—an odd and strange one—but still a restaurant. That guy annoyed me. Maybe it was because he looked like Fredo Corleone from *The Godfather*—a weak, unnecessary pawn. From the look of that place, I expected Fredo's murderous father, Vito, to come out any minute.

But I kept my mafia assumptions to myself.

Jimmy told them we were there to meet Bowie. The man looked in his notebook and then nodded. We were in.

He took us to the back of the restaurant, down a long hallway into the kitchen, then through a pair of hanging white curtains at the end of the kitchen, then through another door in the back. When we entered, David and his friend Coco immediately stood up and shook our hands, pulling us over to some chairs. Coco asked for menus as David and Jimmy immediately launched into an intense discussion about the album that David was working on.

Trying as hard as possible not to stare passionately at Bowie and to maintain an air of composure, I turned my head and looked around. It was near impossible.

I sipped my water and leaned in next to Jimmy as they talked, trying to seem like I was a part of the conversation. Bowie looked exquisite—he wore a plain but spit-clean blue shirt open at the collar and pressed gray slacks. Simple. Dignified. As I sipped my water silently but feverishly, I couldn't help noticing his chest through his open shirt. My gut seized up. I gulped and started to not breathe. Jimmy looked at me.

"You okay, honey?"

I shook.

"Yeah, yeah," I whispered. A cough cracked through my throat. I was becoming too obvious.

I turned away. The room was empty except for the single large round table at which we were seated, and all of the windows were covered by long gilded curtains. My eyes wandered around. This was a cloister. It was safe. It was closed. It was covert. That was why he was here. I imagined all the other people out there, in the front room, had come here to disappear into this sanctuary, too. They could eat upscale Italian cuisine, secluded and sheltered from the outside world. Thing was, to me, it felt more like a prison.

Jimmy ordered the meatballs and I got the chicken marsala. After a few minutes of remarks about the size and weight of the dinners, David looked over at me.

"I met you at Debbie's place, didn't I?" he said.

"Yes," I carefully replied. My stomach wobbled. I put my hand on it.

"You're the drummer, right?" he asked.

Jimmy looked at me, snickering in an annoyingly paternalistic way.

"Yeah, I play the drums for a local band called the Student Teachers," I said.

A sharp pain dug into my gut. I wasn't going to make it through this.

"Right, right, Jimmy was telling me about them." Bowie took a sip of his wine. "I'd like to come and see you. Are you playing soon?"

I gulped. I wasn't sure.

"Uh, yeah, but I'll have to let you know. I have to ask my manager," I said, holding my now throbbing stomach.

"Great!" He looked at Coco. "We're in New York for a while, right?"

Coco nodded. Bowie turned back to me.

"Let me know." He smiled at me and winked.

I smiled back. My gut dropped as I desperately tried to keep sitting peacefully and appearing self-possessed. David Bowie wanted to see my band. In what universe was I traveling? Was this real?

After dinner, Bowie took us in his limousine across town to Radio City Music Hall. We weren't there to see a show, certainly; it was way too late for that. We ended up going into a backdoor entrance, where David talked to someone in a room off to the side of the stage. Immediately, we were escorted to an elevator behind the stage that was as ornate and golden as the ones in the front of the theater. The elevator took us to the top floor and I remember walking down a hallway through huge copper double doors. They opened into a vast, brilliant space filled with art deco furniture and 1920s art. It was dazzling.

After taking in the remarkable sight, I was struck by the silence of the place. It wasn't a regular silence. I ran my hand across the top of a russet-colored deco chest of drawers and there was no dust. I sniffed and checked more of the pieces peppered across the floor. Someone was cleaning this place regularly. But no one seemed to live there. I felt myself shiver from the emptiness of life in that place, or the eccentricity of it.

A few moments later, Jimmy bounced onto one of the couches and took out a white packet and shook out a bunch of lines of coke onto a glass coffee table. He was laughing and joking around with David, who joined him as they sniffed it up. I looked over and noticed there was nowhere to sit except next to Bowie.

"Get over here, honey," Jimmy said.

I reluctantly snuck next to David, who was lighting a cigarette. Jimmy handed me the rolled-up bill and I sniffed up a line. I sat there not wanting to move but really wanting to move at the same time. David and Jimmy were discussing the *Saturday Night Live* show David was set to do and the possibility of Jimmy playing keyboards with him.

I listened, but mostly I sat there, acutely aware of the small bit of air between Bowie and me, of how close I was, of how I had dreamed, as a tiny teen adoring her idol, of being that near him. He was literally six inches away from my left hip. I could smell him. The scent from him was so intensely intoxicating I thought I would faint. It was warm and succulent, like a luscious vanilla ice cream cone covered in hard, tasty chocolate or the waft of the serene air that hits you when you enter a newly cleaned and shining hotel room, throwing you into a blissful sleep as you sink onto the bed. I tried brutally hard not to fall over into his lap.

We hung out at Radio City for a while, until the guard who had brought us up earlier came in and told us the building was closing. I checked my watch. It was near midnight. We went to the lobby and waited as Coco hailed a cab, which took us to the building where Bowie was staying on the West Side. It looked like a regular apartment building, but it was actually an exclusive apartment-hotel—secretive, separate, shielded.

I learned later that the gorgeous art deco apartment in Radio City had been owned by Samuel "Roxy" Rothafel, famous theater impresario, and that after he died in 1936, no one had taken it over. It was a living coffin, rarely seen by many. And if you think about it, it wasn't strange at all that Bowie was one of the few who knew about it or about the back room behind the kitchen at Frankie and Johnnie's. That was the world he lived in, the world he had to live in.

As much time as we spent with him, it was rarely outside, on the street. Whenever we were outdoors, it was merely to go from point A to point B and usually by private car, though sometimes we traveled by taxi. And then David kept his head low in the back. What would happen if the driver, or anyone, saw him? It was never discussed but it was understood that when you were with him, the way the evening or event was structured was always according to what was safest for him. It wasn't that he didn't want to talk to people. The problem was that too many wanted to talk to him. There was no taking a walk on the street with Bowie for an ice cream or a hot dog. Until the last time I saw him.

22

ROOF PARTY

THE STUDENT TEACHERS STARTED HAVING REHEARSALS at a studio on Twelfth Street. I remember thinking that was great because it was right down the street from the New School and I had started taking another course there in European literature.

We were getting ready for a show at Max's with Crayola and had been working on a new song called "Roof Party."[1] And, even more exciting, a new member had joined us. His name was Joe Katz and he had floppy brown hair with a boyish, twinkly face, which curiously obscured his terrific skill playing the guitar. He was playing with the Mumps at this time as well, because they needed someone on bass, another instrument he played. We had initially brought him on with us because Philip was having trouble. He was getting too friendly with his drinking, and it was starting to pull him down. During the day, Joe worked as a mailman. He had been on the scene for a while. He was one of our biggest fans. We liked him and discovered that he made us sound so much better.[2]

Around this time, we were invited by Blondie to be their guest on NBC's *The Midnight Special*. We couldn't believe this sudden opportunity, and it was all because of Jimmy's belief in us. We had started rehearsing madly in preparation, when, a few days before the show, we were informed

---

1 Lori and David seem to remember that we were rehearsing our song "Samantha."

2 Joe and Jody ended up getting married in 1984, are still happily wed, and have a son.

The new cute addition. (PHOTO BY STEVE LOMBARDI)

that NBC had changed their mind about letting us appear, for the single reason that we weren't signed to a major label yet but were only on a smaller independent one. Roy Carr of the *New Musical Express* reported on the struggle Blondie had with NBC over our appearance with them:

It's late afternoon. Clem Burke is now standing in the middle of Debbie Harry and Chris Stein's recently acquired Manhattan rooftop apartment, hanging on the telephone and patiently attempting to placate organist Jimmy Destri who is blowing his top on the other end of the receiver, somewhere way across town. The gist of the conversation, which eventually involves everyone present, is that Destri is arguing that having had to fight against all odds to attain the position they now hold, Blondie should, on principle, pull out of hosting a forthcoming NBC-TV Midnight Special, unless the Student Teachers (a band Destri produces) are not immediately re-instated on Blondie's original list of personally-invited performing guest artists.

So far, Blondie have managed to get Robert Fripp booked onto this prime-time programme (quite an achievement in itself), but the NBC top brass are resisting the inclusion of the Student Teachers.

Surprisingly enough, this decision has nothing to do with their music (which is not unsimilar to Blondie's), or the fact that they're relatively unknown, it's that their only record to date has been a one-off single for the small independent New York Ork label. For reasons best known to themselves, NBC-TV avoid featuring artists without a long-term major label tie-up.

"As they're currently looking for a new deal, to put them on the show right now would imply payola," Debbie hollers across the room to Burke who, like the rest of Blondie, fully sympathize with Destri's motives, but who continues to argue that, at this crucial juncture in their own career, they don't wield sufficient power to dictate terms to a national network as big as NBC.

Chris Stein takes over the phone from Burke and suggests that, if he still feels so adamant about the Student Teachers being dropped, Destri should contact their newly-acquired manager, Shep Gordon, and see if he can apply more pressure on Blondie's behalf. However, Stein continues, as much as he himself would like the Student Teachers on the *Midnight Special*, for Blondie to pull out could prove detrimental to their own career. The aftermath, he suggests, could prove far-reaching.[3]

It was disheartening to all of us except I remember feeling some relief—were we really ready for that?—and the warmth that Blondie showed in wanting to help us, despite their continuing hard work toward success, was heartwarming. On a more personal level, Jimmy's faith in us made me swoon.

One night, while we were rehearsing "Roof Party," the door to the studio suddenly opened. It was Jimmy and Bowie, with Coco behind them.[4] Joe started twanging out "Ziggy Stardust," and it took all the strength I had not to drop my jaw to the floor and to keep the drumsticks from flying out of my hands smack into the back of Lori's head.

---

3 Roy Carr, "Skinny Ties Over America: Blondie's Battle for US Survival," *New Musical Express*, September 29, 1979, pp. 36–39.

4 Bill says that I knew Bowie was coming to the rehearsal, because I had forewarned him. I don't remember this.

We continued playing as they wandered in. Jimmy was beaming so forcefully that I worried he might explode, while Bowie stood there with his hands on his hips, examining us. He moved closer to the stage as we continued the song. It looked like he was eyeing Lori's fingering as she played a riff on the bass; then he turned his head to Joe, on second guitar. He didn't start moving to the beat or snapping his fingers. He just studied us.

I remember trying to be as perfect as possible and not look at him, but to keep playing as the professional musician I was, or was supposed to be. I noticed, since we had started practicing the song from earlier, that it had picked up, felt better, sounded better. After another minute, we finished the song, although for a brief nanosecond, we all froze and stared at Bowie. I kept wishing I had a special camera or some techno device to allow me to freeze that moment and preserve it somewhere in an alternate timeline so I could revisit it later.

Jimmy sang out: "Hey, guys, this is David! David, these are the Student Teachers—David, Bill, Philip, Lori, Joe, and Laura, of course."

"Hey," Bowie said, smiling; then suddenly he jumped onto the stage and stood next to Lori. He started to retune her bass while she stood there holding it, whispering instructions to her, showing her a different way to play the last chord sequence.

"Play it again," he said, jumping off the stage.

I counted off—one, two, three—and we restarted the song. I could hear a slight difference in Lori's riff. And even the rest of us whom Bowie didn't specifically talk to—we were tighter, with more awareness of where we were going with the song. I remember David, specifically, singing with more conviction, more feeling.[5]

After we finished the last stanza, Bowie smiled and clapped. Then Jimmy jumped in.

"Are you guys finished? Because we have to get going," he said, as he handed Philip a beer and lit Lori's cigarette. "David has to get uptown," he continued.

---

5 David says: "I also remember desperately wanting his approval of me as a front man . . . which I didn't really get. He squinted at me . . . like he was summing me up and was going to say something. But to the best of my memory, he never did."

I edged out from behind the drums and picked my bag up off the couch in the corner. As I put on my jacket, I saw Bowie talking to the rest of the guys. It seemed like he really enjoyed the song, like he might work with us. My heart quivered. I edged over next to him as he talked with the band. Could he be interested in us?

I had felt for so long, as I followed Jimmy and Blondie on tour and backstage at their concerts and television appearances, that I was something less. On top of that, it was hard work making music and playing in a band. There are sacrifices and scrapes, there are arguments about how the songs should be played and which songs should be performed or recorded. There are failures and successes. There are a lot of drugs and a lot of sex and a lot of sickness and a lot of struggle, sometimes between bandmates and sometimes involving outside forces. But when I turned around after putting on my jacket, and saw everyone talking heatedly with Bowie, all the struggle and infighting melted away. The sense I'd always had that I was a C- actor in the movie starring Jimmy and Blondie started to dissipate. We were good enough for Bowie, it seemed. For that moment, at least.

"What's good about this song is it will catch people," Bowie said. "You need to catch people," he continued and lit a cigarette.

Everybody heard him. Except they weren't breathing. I knew they were stuck inside a tightly sealed flask of their own disbelief. I was in there with them.

Bowie then went over to Joe and lifted Joe's guitar over his head and draped it over himself. He played Joe's chord sequence perfectly after only having heard it twice.

"I know what you're doing here," he said to Joe. He played the chord sequence Joe normally performed.

"I hope you don't mind me sticking my prick where it doesn't belong," he said[6] as he replayed Joe's chord line with a slight change in the notes, then looked at Philip.

"This won't change your lead," he said.

---

6 Joe remembers that Bowie told me that Joe was an "eyesore." He says he plans to get a tattoo of that.

Then he played Joe's line again and it sounded deeper, broader. As he talked with Joe and Lori[7] more about their parts, it occurred to me he was focusing on the support instruments, the backstory, the instrument lines that held up the song. I figured it was because he liked "Roof Party" the way it was, that he thought it was a good song. But he wanted to enlarge it, make it even bigger and better.

I remember wondering why he didn't say anything to me about the supporting backstory for the song. I was the drummer and, well, if any instrument was the foundation of a song, it was the drums. But he never said anything to me about how I played the drums. Thinking about it later, I realized it was because, ultimately, I was just a metronome. A metronome is what it is, no more.

After he finished working with Joe, he bumped over to the keyboard and played a chord sequence change there. He suggested Bill hold down a weird chord on the Elka to go under the ending section and then put his hands on Bill's to show him how to do it.[8] He then took his hands off the keys while Bill, manically nodding his head yes, replayed it. Bill stared at his keys and replayed Bowie's sequence a few more times. I know Bill was both trying to memorize it while asking himself if he was playing it as well as Bowie had—if it would ever be as good.

Bowie then jumped off the stage and Coco gave him his coat.

"When's the next gig guys?" Jimmy asked. I zipped up my jacket. We all glanced at Jody, who was sitting quietly in the corner. She quickly checked her notebook.

"The nineteenth at Irving Plaza," she dutifully reported through her smile.

Everybody started packing up, and Jimmy, David, and I headed for the door. Just before we left, Bowie raced over to Jody. I learned later he had suggested to her that the rhythm section be moved to the front of the stage next to David. I assumed it was because we were a female rhythm section and there weren't many of those around rock 'n' roll at the time.

---

7   David says: "I do recall him standing closely behind Lori and showing her something she could do on the bass . . . not a clue what it was, but the look on her face stays with me: half disbelieving thrill, half trembling terror!"

8   Philip says that's something you can actually hear if you listen to a recording of "Roof Party"—this weird, arty, spacey, dissonant jazz chord on top of the guitar parts in the outro.

If nothing else, Bowie was a businessman. He knew how to get attention. He knew what worked.

One week later, Jody got a call from concert promoter Jonny Podell[9] and was told we were scheduled to open for the Cramps and Iggy Pop at the Palladium on Halloween, and at the club My Father's Place in Long Island, three days later. Although Jody, through her tireless negotiating, had been talking with Podell about a gig with the Cramps specifically, she hadn't had a lot of luck with him. But then, just one week after Bowie had reworked our song at rehearsal, we were on the schedule. Everyone knew of Iggy Pop's legendary connection with Bowie. Just before the gig was announced and advertised, Jimmy told me that Bowie had greased those Podell wheels.

The difference between the Palladium and My Father's Place was obvious. Although the Palladium was an enormous concert hall, worlds larger than any venue we had ever played in, My Father's Place was still a club. However, it was an enormous one—another stop far larger than we had ever known. But those were the steps a band took to get more exposure and more success—hopefully. For that time, for that week, that's how it felt to us. We were climbing up the ladder—we were getting somewhere.

We didn't see Iggy much at the Palladium gig, but we did get a chance to hang with him at My Father's Place. Jimmy knew Iggy from past shows Blondie had performed with him, and they were like two old high school buddies hanging out, getting a couple of brews and talking about the latest Knicks game.

The dressing rooms at My Father's Place were downstairs and it was a zoo down there, between all the guys in Iggy's band, us, and all of Iggy's fans, girlfriends, wannabes, and hangers-on. It was fun but distracting and, not unlike at the Palladium, we didn't perform at our best, or even near it. We had been wildly thrown by the sudden call to play these bigger, more mainstream venues, and were caught completely off guard. In fact, despite our small dedicated fan base in the front row at My Father's Place, the larger part of the audience didn't like us much and ended up tossing food at us—slices of pizza, french fries, half-eaten burgers. As Lori mused, at least we were fed.

---

9   Podell was also Blondie's booking agent.

After the last set of the night, we were in our dressing room downstairs, and Jimmy slipped in with Iggy. He introduced us, and it was so energizing, so cool to meet him. Iggy was always associated with Bowie, not just because Bowie was a fan of Iggy's first band, the Stooges, but they had really liked each other and had become fast friends. Yet in so many ways Iggy was very different from Bowie, and that may have been why Bowie was drawn to him. The difference wasn't just in the kind of music they made, where Iggy's was raunchier and more dirty compared with Bowie's more cerebral colors, but it showed even in the way they dressed and walked. Bowie was more refined, even reserved, while Iggy was more street, though in a very unpredictable, sexy way. Either way, Bowie craved what he didn't know. You can see it in his music and all his artistic adventures. He was always hungry.

I remember Jimmy acting as animated and vibrant as ever when he came in with Iggy behind him. He adored Iggy and was really excited that we were playing these shows with him. A moment later, about six people barreled in. They were all friends of Iggy's, and within minutes, white packets of coke were being passed around. While hanging out with Iggy shocked us all, David was particularly thrown when Iggy told him Frank Sinatra was one of his favorite singers. David said he couldn't reconcile his idol admiring his mother's heartthrob (she had been a bobby-soxer). Then Iggy told a few tales of the Stooges days and Jimmy said he should write a book. Iggy's reply was as poignant as it was insistent:

"No. I'm a singer. I'm not a writer. I'm not an actor. I don't play guitar. I'm not a producer. I'm just a singer. That's it."

Although he went on to write and act, he was firm about that then. And his interest at that moment was not in us, but in our darling resident go-go dancer, Ellen.

Although the bright lights of the exploding world of big-time rock 'n' roll—even in its embryonic stages for us at the Palladium and My Father's Place—were intoxicating, there was a problem stewing within us. It wasn't that any of us necessarily believed we couldn't ultimately make it. The problem was internal. It was a standing pot of cold water on the stove as the flame is lit and the water slowly starts warming up, bubbling and bubbling, the temperature rising. I thought about that rising temperature as I got in the car with Jimmy afterward and Iggy joined us, and I worried about the fallout, once the water hit boiling.

23

TITULAR

BOWIE WAS WORKING ON HIS NEXT ALBUM, which was to be called *Scary Monsters (and Super Creeps)*. He was recording it at the Power Station on the West Side of Manhattan. Like Blank Tape Studios, the Power Station was a cave stuck inside a windowless portal where no time or space existed.

Jimmy had been asked to play keyboards with Bowie in his appearance on *Saturday Night Live* in mid-December, and he was at the Power Station a lot rehearsing with him for the show. Bowie planned to perform three songs with Klaus Nomi and Joey Arias as backup. He was putting down tracks for the *Scary Monsters* album while doubling his time with rehearsals.

I spent a lot of time sitting in the recording studio watching Bowie and his engineer. Jimmy was in and out as he bounced between helping Bowie with some of the producing and rehearsing for the *SNL* show. I noticed Klaus Nomi springing around as well. There was a specific sense of urgency and delicacy around everyone, a feeling that something remarkable was happening and being created. I always sensed that energy emanating around Bowie. No matter where he was or what he was doing, there was always a possibility, a risk of some kind of mysterious treasure building within.

Saturday Night Live was recorded at 30 Rockefeller Center in midtown, as it is today. It was an amazing feeling edging into that iconic, legendary building, taking the gold-trimmed art deco elevator up to the set on the eighth floor. It was even more shocking to my system to be escorted through the double doors backstage, past the lines of waiting audience members. I was silent and gripped, absorbing everything I saw. I prayed I might see Gilda Radner or John Belushi, but being as close as I was to them at that moment nearly toppled me.

Jimmy and I were with Blondie's road manager, Bruce, and we were immediately set up in a dressing room down the hall from the green room. I remember going for a short walk through the backstage hallway, making sure I moved with some authority so it appeared I belonged there. At the end of the hall to the right there was a big dressing room filled with makeup artists working on actors from the cast. I quickly looked to see if I recognized anyone, but I had to be careful or else I would seem like some kind of psycho stalker. But my brief glance caught none of the big actors like Bill Murray or Jane Curtin. As I swiftly walked back to the dressing room, though, Gilda Radner went past me in a costume for one of her skits. I really wanted to tell her how amazing she was but I couldn't. I would get in too much trouble being where I shouldn't be anyway.

I grabbed a soda from the cooler in the hallway as I went back to the dressing room. Jimmy was getting his makeup put on and talking with Bruce. I sat down to wait for him to be called. A moment later, Bowie walked in to see how everything was going. Jimmy jumped up and asked him something about the start of "When You're a Boy," and after they coordinated, Bowie quickly left. He had major costume work to get done before they were called onstage.

After a little while, Jimmy went backstage and I headed to the green room to sit out the show. There was a big television in the corner and a window in the wall where we could watch the show live in the auditorium below, since we were on the floor above the studio. No matter what, though, if I had to go anywhere and seek out anything or anyone, I was ordered not to—I was to stay put in the green room.

When Bowie was called to the stage by that night's host, Martin Sheen, he was carried onstage in a life-size marionette costume by Klaus Nomi and Joey Arias. Jimmy was behind two keyboards on stage left and they launched into "The Man Who Sold the World." It was a stunning show and I remember Jimmy trying to deliver a Nomi-esque performance behind the keyboard. That had come from Bowie. He wanted Nomi's otherworldly style everywhere onstage, even from performers not in the front. Bowie always brought his unique and demanding slant to bear in regard to every single aspect of his work. Anywhere. I wondered how much of that was him, organically, and how much was just good business.

. ● .

ONE WEEK AFTER *SNL*, JIMMY AND I WERE CATAPULTED onto a short European tour with Blondie. We flew to London the day before Christmas. It would be the first time I hadn't spent Christmas with my Mom and MB. I was really upset about that and resolved to get gifts for them when I was in Scotland. I also had to be back in New York for our gig at Hurrah with the band Unnatural Axe in early January.

On our second day in London, we found ourselves at a BBC television studio. It was huge and spacious, with a small stage in the middle and nothing else—no audience, no director, no fans.

After a little while being there, Debbie and Clem climbed onto the stage, followed by Jimmy and Chris and Nigel. There were no amps or cords anywhere and the drums were in the front of the stage, next to Debbie. She was wearing a knee-length black-and-white striped dress, looking stunning, as everyone got in place to perform "Sunday Girl." I stood backstage biting my fingernails off.

It was *Top of the Pops*.

My eyes moved around the entire place. I was frantic, shaking, bursting with the realization of the history of that stage. It was fantastic reliving, in my mind, when the Beatles had played one of their first appearances on *Top of the Pops*: sparse set with John, Paul and George separate from one another—no amps, no wires, and Ringo up front on the stage, like Clem was now with Debbie. That was *Top of the Pops*, and history was weighing on everyone in a nearly unspeakable way. But Blondie carried it and was completely inside the *Top of the Pops* scheme. They had it.

While we were in London, we visited Abbey Road Studios. It was hard not to be completely thrown by it all, yet Jimmy didn't seem nearly as impressed. I think it was hard for him to step back and look at the history of the Beatles and how they'd laid out the framework Jimmy was using to write hit songs, how they'd blazed the path he was traveling. His mind was fogged up by Blondie's soaring success. "Heart of Glass" had hit number one in the U.S. by that time, and had been at the top of the charts in the UK earlier that year. The aftermath was a fast and raging triumph that blinded all of them, but mostly Jimmy.

A tour bus was arranged for all of us to use, because the shows were throughout England, on the way to Glasgow, Scotland, for a New Year's Eve performance at the Apollo theater. Before we left London, we visited a nightclub in Piccadilly Square. The most remarkable thing about it was the intense revelry of everyone there. The costumes, the decorations, the music, the lights—it was more celebratory than anything I had ever seen in my life, even Studio 54 back in New York. This was the first time I saw such concentrated, staggering partying. The club was packed and people danced everywhere, not just inside the swaying crowds but on the bar, hanging from the ceiling, bouncing off the walls—it was a true *Clockwork Orange*.

As I stood at the bar, sandwiched between costumed revelers, Jimmy pulled me away from the madness to a corner underneath a staircase. He introduced me to a guy standing there. His name was Doug Fieger—he had a drink in his hand and his arm around a beautiful young woman with glossy dark hair.

"Honey, this is Doug Fieger, lead singer of the Knack," Jimmy said, jumping and laughing.

The Knack! Wow! I said to myself. Their song "My Sharona" was on every chart in the world. I shook his hand and smiled.

"And this," Jimmy gestured to the pretty young girl with Doug, "is Sharona."

I was astonished.

"Wow! Great to meet you!" I said.

We all started talking and hanging together like we were the best of friends. We ended up going out to the London clubs together for the next two nights before Blondie's tour bus took off. The most terrific thing about hanging with Doug and Sharona Alperin was how close we four got in such a short time, and I think it was because Sharona and I were the same age and Doug and Jimmy were the same age. We felt like comrades. Despite the enormous fame they were facing with the Knack's

"My Sharona" and Jimmy's celebrity with Blondie, that time in London with Doug and Sharona was easy and fun—and near normal.

· ● ·

THE TOUR BUS BLONDIE USED TO GET TO GLASGOW was massive. There were four large bunk beds in the back and a big TV hanging at the front, which, at first glance, seemed really cool but became increasingly annoying to me.

I had gotten an extension on the final paper for my European lit class at the New School and I'd figured I would try to write the bulk of it on that bus ride to Glasgow, so a blaring TV above my head didn't help. Of course, there were daily stops for more shows at Bournemouth, Manchester, and Birmingham, but I planned to keep working on the paper backstage. It was due the day I returned to New York in early January. I had to finish it.

Glasgow was a crazy experience, not only because of the Scottish realm with the sweeping mountain ranges surrounding it, the stark blue sky above it, and the remarkable Victorian buildings everywhere, but because of the raging Blondie fans who attacked the band when the bus drove up in front of the hotel. Blondie had always been a huge success in the UK, far greater than in the U.S., but nothing prepared me for what greeted us in Glasgow.

Security guards and Scottish police had to barricade the crowds before we could get off the bus, and we had to wait for what seemed like hours inside the vehicle before it was all brought under control. When we were finally able to get off, the police escorted us into the hotel. We were quickly taken to our rooms to avoid any fans who might have escaped into the lobby.

When we got upstairs and unpacked, everyone wandered into each other's rooms talking about the heavy attention and how to handle it. It felt far more nerve-racking than if we were home. We were away from our known and protected environment, even though the Scottish police were outside—it was just not home.

When I was with Blondie on tour, or even out on small East Coast excursions with my own band, hotel life, and sheltered hotel life at that, was the new normal. Although it was initially exciting and titillating, it very soon lost its charm.

Temporary life is no real life, and the problem with the world inhabited by the famous and stars of entertainment, rock 'n' roll, politics, etc., is that it's colored by constant travel and constant impermanence. After a while, it starts to corrode your spirit. It's worse when you're surrounded with the kind of fame that Blondie and Bowie experienced, because, in that case, the impermanent life also becomes one where deception reigns. They had to delude the world in order to survive in it.

Luckily, because I was an unknown, I could leave the Glasgow hotel room and go outside. Normally Jimmy would have come with me, but the fanaticism of the Blondie fans was too intense, so he stayed in the hotel. The next afternoon, I dragged Bruce with me to walk through the historic Scottish streets. After we visited the Kelvingrove Art Gallery and Museum, Bruce told me he had to get to the Apollo for sound check. I hurried back with him, but I quickly stopped at a sweater shop and picked up a handmade sweater for my mom. It was made of sheep's wool in varying shades of dark beige and maroon. Then I grabbed a knitted Scottish bag for MB.

The midnight, New Year's Eve Apollo show was packed. Debbie was stunning and the band was on fire. The entire show was broadcast live, on the BBC, and the place was filled with TV cameras and crew. It was really exciting.

Because we hit the time of the New Year six hours earlier than the U.S., as soon as I could pull myself away from the Blondie after-party backstage, I dashed back to the hotel room to call my mom.

"Happy New Year, Mom!" I cried. "How are you?"

"I'm fine, dear heart. Are you okay? What has it been like over there?"

"It's been great. How was Christmas? Did you go out to the farm and see Granddaddy?"

"Yes. He asked about you and I told him you were in Europe for the holidays. He was so happy for you," she said. "Are you okay?"

I stopped.

"Honey, are you there?" she asked.

Suddenly, the international operator came on and warned me I had fifteen seconds left on my call.

"Honey, are you there? Are you having a happy New Year?" Mom asked.

"Yes, Mom . . . yes."

Then the phone clicked. I put the receiver down. I stared at it. I really missed her. For that instant, and despite the thrill of everything, it felt wrong that I was in Europe and not with her.

A moment later the door swung open. It was Jimmy.

"Hey, baby! Happy New Year!" He was drunk. He came over and sat down next to me.

"There's another party downstairs. Wanna go?"

"Not really," I said. I grabbed a cigarette.

Jimmy reached over and started unbuttoning my blouse.

I stopped him.

"Not right now, okay?" I said. I started to light my cigarette.

He ignored me.

"What are you talking about?" he said, his voice starting to rise. He pulled on my shirt and grabbed at the zipper on my jeans. I stood up quickly.

"Not now, all right? I'm tired," I said—and I was. I had drunk too much champagne and, well, I missed my family.

Jimmy immediately got up after me and grabbed at my shirt again.

"Jimmy!" I screamed. "Stop!"

Suddenly he whacked me with the back of his hand and I fell down. I grabbed my face and rubbed it. I looked up at him. I couldn't believe it. What was happening? He sat down on the bed and dragged his hand over his eyes.

"I'm so sorry," he said.

Then he got up and walked out the door.

I stayed on the floor. I pulled my knees up into myself while I rubbed my cheek. What was happening? I started crying, and tightly wrapped my arms around myself. I tried to think why Jimmy had done that to me. Then I thought about that time he'd banged his head on the wall after doing some cocaine. It was getting worse.

24

MACHIAVELLIAN

WHEN I GOT BACK TO NEW YORK in early January '79, I met the band for rehearsal at Twelfth Street. Jimmy wasn't due back until the end of the month, so I was on my own at the Jones Street apartment and for the moment that was fine. Plus, MB came over and stayed with me so we could be two grown-up women taking on the big city in our own place, in between fudge pops, popcorn, and our favorite shows, *Taxi* and *Rhoda*.

The Student Teachers hadn't played together for nearly a month, and we had gigs scheduled every weekend during the next one. We really needed to get back on track. On the way to our first rehearsal, I stopped at the New School and dropped off my paper in the office. It was on Leo Tolstoy's *The Death of Ivan Ilyich*, and as much as I adored the book, my paper went nowhere. I was really disappointed with it.

But it was great seeing the guys again. It had been too long. When I went into the studio, I saw Lori lighting up and lounging and David and Philip going over a new song, while Joe and Bill wandered around the stage testing their instruments, and Jody and Antone hung out in the corner. The scene was a dollop of buttery mashed potatoes. Comfort.

After I set up my drums and ran my sticks across them, Philip and Joe tuned up, Lori jumped up on the stage, and David quickly engaged us.

"'The Second Before,' guys," he called out. "Let's do it."

We immediately started playing. Then we played "Roof Party" and "Past Tense."

About a half hour later, after we had gone through about four or five songs, I started to feel my arms tiring. I still kept up the beat, and when

I looked at everyone else, no one was looking back at me like I wasn't keeping up, even though I felt fatigue start to course throughout my body. I thought to myself, as I struggled to get the rhythm out, that I had been drinking too much and doing too much coke. I worried I was skipping a beat. My thoughts, as I played, weren't confused, but foggy. I looked at the guys again. They were all busy playing, focusing, and concentrating. The song sounded good. I just didn't feel good.

A few days later, when Jimmy got home from the European tour, he literally crashed for two days. He went into a dead sleep and didn't even take a sandwich or a soda when I brought them up to him. Finally, when he arose from beneath the tomb of the bed's blankets, he seemed brighter and certainly happier than when I'd last seen him. It was strange that he hadn't contacted me much while he was away. I just figured we were both too busy and that we would reconnect now that he was back.

That weekend, we played at Hurrah, opening for the Know, again. The show went super well, and after our set, as the rest of the band raced to the front of the club to watch the Know play, I hung back by the bar with Jimmy and Robert Boykin. They were gabbing about Blondie's Glasgow show, and Jimmy and I were laughing at the intensity of the fans at the hotel when suddenly I heard behind me:

"Yeah, and they were worse in Paris!"

I turned around. It was that mousy girlfriend of Eddie's.

I gave Jimmy a hard look.

"Hey, Jess!" he said and took my hand.

"Jess and Eddie were at the Paris shows, honey," he said meekly, but with pushy energy. "We had a great time!"

He turned to Jess.

"Did you guys end up going to the Eiffel Tower?" he asked her.

I took my hand away from Jimmy's and walked to one of the dressing rooms. There were some people doing their makeup by the mirror. I didn't know them. I sat down. Thinking. Thinking. Thinking. He'd had that affair with her last year and now she'd apparently been at a show when I wasn't there. Also, I knew that Eddie rarely, if ever, left his apartment. He was a drug dealer, dammit. Remaining home—undercover—was a job requirement.

Suddenly, the dressing room door swung open. Jimmy walked in and stood there, eyeing me.

"What are you doing?" he asked abruptly.

"Why is she here?"

"I don't know. It's a fucking free country! I guess she's here to see you guys and the Know!" he snapped back.

"Where's Eddie?"

"Home, I guess," he said. "What does it matter?"

Home. Of course he was home. He never left home.

"Never mind," I said, and went back to the bar.

. . .

A FEW WEEKS LATER, WE HEADLINED AT CBGB for three nights. Although we had headlined at various clubs before, including out of town in Boston and Philadelphia, this was our first three-night gig where we were the headline act, and it felt terrific. We had evolved, both musically and with enough of a fan base, to the point that being the main draw made sense to us and to the booking agents as well. It didn't freak us out or make us nervous. We were there, we had it, and we could make the show great. Even as we lugged in our equipment with Antone and Jody, we felt like old-timers. We had been there so many times before—the planks on the stage floor creaked where they always had, the dressing room was the same grubby area, the graffiti on the bathroom walls downstairs was the same. I even leaned over the top of CB's bar before the sound check and squirted some Pepsi for myself through the nozzle. Home.

Then, when we were onstage, at the beginning of our set—around 10 p.m.—Bowie appeared. We were launching into the first song, "Channel 13," and when I swung around to slam the ride cymbal, I saw him. Jimmy had been doing some work with him and apparently he'd brought Bowie to CB's to see us.

Of course, Bowie had threatened a few times to come to one of our shows, but I'd never believed him. Or rather, I hadn't wanted to believe him. But now he'd followed up on the threat. It was obviously dark and crowded in the club, but it was hard not to notice him. They sat him at a table a few rows back from the stage behind the sound-mixing board, and I waved at him and Coco as we were going into the next song. My blood pressure started spiking. While I played, I watched him—watching us.

I saw Bill was on to him, too, and I was sure David knew Bowie was there. I tried to get Philip and Joe's attention, to see if they saw him, but they were turned away from me. Lori looked unfazed, but I knew she wasn't. What a thrill that was: Him being there made everything worth it—and also reduced it to nothing. Maybe that was the problem. As human as Bowie was, I knew he just wasn't. It was too quixotic, too unreal.

"Well done!" Bowie said to me later, as we climbed into his limousine. He smiled and gave me a big hug.

"They're using the chord change I showed them!" he said cheerfully.

"Yeah," I coughed, smiling nervously. Always nervous.

We were heading uptown, to Studio 54. David wanted a late-night jaunt, and apparently James Brown was filming a performance there.

Even though I had been there before, Studio 54 was still a shock to walk into—it was as grand and as ostentatious as ever. It was more famous than any other club in the city, and the lines to get in were longer and remained there until the moment the club closed and later, even— near 5 a.m. It was as if people had some distant spiritual hope the doors would suddenly open to them, revealing an afterlife of glittery illusions.

It was so difficult to maneuver through the crowds. It was, without fail, always jam-packed, and everyone, whether they were stoned or not, had near out-of-body experiences as they danced and twirled and boogied, flying through the air to the pounding music. The other unique aspect of the place, surpassing all others, was the number of celebrities who always wandered around or were sitting at the tables. I must've caught a glimpse of Warhol and Mick Jagger and Keith Richards every time I was there. It's just the way it was at Studio 54.

That night, James Brown was bursting into flames. I think it was planned to be one of his last performances—for a while at least—and he performed like it was, even though each of his performances always seemed like his last. The place was teeming with James Brown fanatics. After we got inside the club, one of the concierges escorted us to a table where there was privacy. As Bowie was with us, that was required.

But before we were all seated, I took off to the central dance floor. Brown was belting out "Sex Machine" and sweating buckets onto everyone. The crowd was dancing in mass unison to his music, and their force shook the entire building. I squeezed between as many bodies as I could, finally getting near the stage to watch him. The King of Soul. It was mesmerizing seeing that legend who, like Elvis, the Beatles, and the Rolling Stones, had laid the groundwork for all of us. It was hard to move from the small place, at the foot of the stage, as he banged out another great one, his latest hit, "Take a Look at Those Cakes."

The crowd exploded and I was nearly crushed. I squeezed my way back to the table, struggling through the compressed wet bodies. Bowie and Jimmy were in heated discussion again, and there was coke on the table—again. I sat down and gulped down some water. I was as wet as James Brown looked back there. Jimmy grabbed my hand.

"I was just telling David about your dad," he said.

I spit my water back out.

"What?" I squeezed out of my throat.

"Your dad—art critic for *Newsweek*," he said. "I was telling David he could talk to him—that he could look over David's paintings."

I put my glass down on the table.

"What do you think?" Jimmy asked.

I swallowed.

"Sure, uh, that sounds great," I said.

Except it didn't.

My dad could be, at best, challenging. But if there was one thing he loved, it was fame, and how could I ever deny David Bowie?

About two hours later, we left and took Bowie's limo to his building. He and Coco got out and after he shut the car door, he pointed at us.

"Dinner! Tomorrow!" He smiled and turned away.

Jimmy looked at me.

I sank back into the car seat and looked out the window. The limo started up and I watched the streetlights fly by. Not many cars out at 4 a.m.

After a moment, however, the streetlights started dragging and the glow didn't stop after we passed them. It lasted, streaking. I blinked. I looked again. The car came to a stop at Thirty-Fifth Street, and the post office building, on the corner, looked double. There were two of them. I shook my head, then opened my eyes and looked around. Everything was in double.

25

MARILYN ALWAYS KNEW

THE NEXT MORNING WHEN MY EYELIDS SQUEAKED OPEN, I immediately sat up and looked around me. No double vision. I heaved a massive sigh. I laid back down. I had to stop with the cocaine. It was starting to have a bad effect on me—I was sure of it.

Jimmy snored next to me. I looked over at the alarm clock. It was 3 p.m. Fuck. There was no sunlight in my life anymore. I was getting so tired of losing every day. I looked back at Jimmy. It was no loss to him. Day or night, sunset or sunrise—it was all the same to him, because as far as he was concerned, we existed only in a bubble. It was always 11:59 for us, and it would never change.

Except it always did.

Later, after I came out of the shower, I saw that Jimmy was awake and having a cigarette in the living room. He was on the phone. It was with Bowie, he told me later. They were going to meet us at the loft in SoHo—where I'd grown up—to meet my dad.

I had called my dad before I'd gotten in the shower, and told him Bowie wanted to meet him. He sounded intrigued but also a little confused. He couldn't understand why. I explained to him that Bowie was a pretty accomplished painter, that he was passionate about the visual arts, had been all his life, and that when he'd learned that my dad was the art critic for *Newsweek*, he'd wanted to meet him. Dad hesitated but eventually agreed. I don't think he was as impressed, even in a small way, by the fact that it was David Bowie. I remember thinking it was probably a generation thing. Bowie was the star for my age group, and for my dad it was Elvis Presley, I guess. Even though Dad was married to a woman closer to my age than his, and they had plenty of rock albums in the house—Beatles, the Stones, and Iron Maiden—for some reason, the fact that it was David Bowie didn't resonate.

But even more so, I don't think rock stars possessed the same gravitas for my dad that other well-known figures from other fields such as art, politics, and academia carried for him. When I was eleven years old, he took us with him to Syracuse, New York, to a retrospective show of Yoko Ono's art, because he was reviewing it for *Newsweek*. I think he brought us along because he knew about our obsession with the Beatles and thought we could meet John Lennon. Except he didn't tell us he planned all along to introduce us to Lennon. Even despite my age, I remember that internal shock springing up, the kind you feel when you experience something that either you didn't expect would happen or didn't expect would have such a profound effect. Even at eleven years old, I realized how lucky I was just to shake his hand. It happened outside of our hotel room because John and Yoko were staying at the same hotel and my dad had connected with Yoko that day to set up an interview. When Dad introduced us, and I turned to Lennon, I gulped and then froze. To look up at him and see his face and eyes in real life, where he had only ever been a voice, a picture on the front of an album, an idea, a myth—it's easy to say it was thrilling, but it was light-years beyond that, far beyond. What added to the thrill was that we were able to meet George Harrison and Ringo Starr, on the plane back to New York, the next day. But the bottom line was, despite that earth-shattering moment, my dad was there for Yoko and her art, not for Lennon.

However, Dad adored notoriety, and he relished celebrity. But it had to be the right kind of celebrity. He had known Picasso; he still knew Sturtevant, Lichtenstein, Nam June Paik, even Warhol (although I think they just "tolerated" one another); he was close to Congressman John Brademas and had dinners with Caroline Kennedy and her husband, Ed Schlossberg. These connections charged him, satiated his ego. But for some unknowable reason, the prospect of meeting David Bowie didn't grab him. Nonetheless, dinner it would be.

· ● ·

I ITCHED AND MANGLED MYSELF ON AND OFF THE COUCH in the loft. MB was there, and she was really excited, so that helped me ignore my dad's irritating wonky behavior. It had been a tense half hour with him. We were all sitting on the couches at the far side of the loft, waiting. Dad and Jimmy were drinking Heinekens. Dad was not a fan of Jimmy, even though Jimmy tried very hard to impress him. He told him about Blondie's tour in Europe and how they had filmed 20/20 in Paris. At that, Jane jumped up.

"Oh, *mon Dieu, comment était-ce?*" she said. Jimmy stared at her.

Jane translated: "How was that?" Just then, the buzzer rang in the kitchen. I jumped up, barely catching my tumbling glass of Coca-Cola. I grabbed Jimmy.

"Come on, we have to get him," I gasped, and raced to the intercom. "We'll come get you!" I yelled into it.

We ran to the elevator and pushed the handle to go down. When we got to the lobby and opened the cranking metal doors, Bowie stood there, looking around. Coco was with him.

For an instant, I was punch-drunk. I'd had these same kinds of feelings from time to time during the past year, ever since I first met him. I still experienced the awe of the starstruck teen, yet it was evolving into something else. Whenever he talked, I listened raptly. He didn't just talk about music and the scene and his new album. He talked about politics, philosophy, design. He looked between the lines everywhere. His thoughts were engineered within places in music not many of us went, and that thinking captured me because it went way beyond rock 'n' roll.

So I had to catch myself after the elevator doors opened.

"Hi!" I said, jumping up.

Bowie smiled.

"Didn't John start this place?" he asked me. We all got on the freight elevator. I pushed the crank handle up.

"John?" I asked.

"Lennon," he said. "Didn't Lennon found this building? This cooperative, right?"

We arrived at the fourth floor. I lifted the handle to stop the elevator. Jimmy pushed open the doors.

"Oh yes!" I said. "Yes, he founded it with Yoko and George Maciunas. It's called Fluxhouse," I explained, and showed Bowie and Coco into the loft.

When we turned the corner of the next wall into the main room, I waved to my dad. Jane and MB sprinted over and introduced themselves. They blushed so hard, I was sure their cheeks would crack. My dad pushed himself off the sofa, came over, and bowed in introduction. He always did that. Instead of extending his hand, he bowed down to whoever stood in front of him. That always struck me as strange.

Bowie bowed back to Dad in response. Then, he noticed the Warhol print of Marilyn Monroe on the far wall.

"Ah, you know Andy?"

My dad looked back at the print.

"Yes, yes!" he said. He started to laugh and handed Bowie a Heineken. Bowie took the opened bottle and sat on the floor in the living room.

"But that's not a Warhol," Dad said, coughing. "That's an Elaine Sturtevant print of a Warhol of Marilyn Monroe," he went on, basking in the attention. "But, yes, Andy and I are friends."

Bowie started talking about Berlin with Dad—the city had a strong hold on both of them. Then, suddenly, the phone rang. I quickly ran to the kitchen and grabbed it.

"Hello?"

"Where are you?" It was Philip.

"What? Where?"

"Rehearsal! Right now!" he snapped back.

"What? Now?" I asked.

"Yeah! For the Town Hall gig next week!"

Shit! I had completely forgotten.

"I'm so sorry," I said. "Can we reschedule? I'm here at the loft with Bowie."

"I really doubt it!" he said.

I sighed.

"Philip—"

"Laura, you've missed two rehearsals in the last month."

"Yeah, I know. I'm so sorry," I said. "Can we set up another one for tomorrow?" I asked. "I'll be there, I promise."

"I hope so!" he remarked, and hung up.

I looked over at Dad. He and Bowie were laughing and talking. I touched my head. I felt really tired. Jane came up behind me to stir her beef bourguignon, which was simmering on the stove. I turned around to her. Suddenly there were two Janes stirring the pot. I closed my eyes for a moment, breathed deeply, then opened them. One Jane. One beef bourguignon. Whew, my eyes were okay.

Later, after dinner, Bowie and my dad walked through the rest of the loft, reviewing the other pieces of art hanging on the walls. They were mostly my dad's own work. I know he was likely pleased that Bowie was talking mostly about my dad and his work, although that wasn't why Bowie had come over in the first place. But it wasn't in Dad's purview to take much interest in someone else, unless he had to for work—like when Picasso died in 1973. Dad was on the next jet to France. No, Bowie was not Picasso—though to me, he was close.

After we left, Bowie took us in his limo back to Jones Street. MB was with us and I could hear her gasping under her breath as she squeezed the bones in my hand almost to the breaking point. When we arrived at the apartment, MB and I got out, and as we headed to the front door, I turned, expecting to see Jimmy behind me, but he wasn't there. He had remained in the limo with Bowie. I looked over to them, confused. Had Jimmy said he was staying to hang with Bowie? After a moment, the limo took off.

26

STRINGENT

IN EARLY 1980, WE TREKKED OUT TO WEST ORANGE, New Jersey, to record two singles for Red Star Records. Red Star was owned and run by Marty Thau,[1] believed to be the father of indie rock. He had managed the New York Dolls and coproduced Suicide's first album, *Suicide*.

The album Marty Thau was creating was to include two songs from five different bands: the Fleshtones, the Comateens, the Bloodless Pharaohs, Revelons, and us, the Student Teachers. The album would eventually be called *Marty Thau Presents 2x5*. Jimmy was the producer, and he was more hyped than ever at this recording. He had selected most of the bands for the album, and it was more certain than ever that this was the direction in which he was moving: record producing.

The plan Jimmy had for us was to record the songs "Looks" and "What I Can't Feel." I don't remember preparing for or rehearsing much for this recording, and I wished we had. Maybe because we had been playing for two years already, it wasn't considered necessary. However, the whole thing felt rushed.

Because the cost of the recording studio was high, we convened at House of Music, in West Orange, New Jersey, for a late-night recording, with plans to record both songs in a single night.

We edged into the studio hesitantly, on the verge of serious battle fatigue. Then we noticed that Patti Smith and Robert Fripp had recorded

---

1 Marty Thau is considered one of the five hundred most important record producers in music history and behind-the-scenes heroes of popular music, as cited in Eric Olsen, Paul Verna, Carlo Wolff, *The Encyclopedia of Record Producers* (New York: Billboard Books, 1999).

there, and our nerves busted inside of themselves. For the moment, we were rejuvenated.

We ended up recording at what felt like supersonic speed because we only had about seven or eight hours in the studio. One of the new things we did this time around was add backup vocals. It was for the song "Looks," and although it's disputed who came up with the idea, I was one of the backup singers, along with Lori and Philip,[2] and that was some of the most fun I'd had in a long time. Being the drummer sometimes can feel very empty—you do what's required, then go sit in the waiting room until the song is finished. Singing backup on "Looks" made me feel more a part of the recording process than I ever had before.

We finished in the studio around 5 a.m. and climbed into Antone's van for the journey home. What an overwhelming, hard-pushing job that was—laying down two songs in seven hours, and whether we had done a good job was highly questionable.

. ● .

A FEW WEEKS LATER, JIMMY AND I WERE AT HURRAH. Suicide were on the stage, and Robert Boykin was hosting a bunch of investors, including Pat Gibbons, who was Bowie's business manager. Because Robert had become good friends with Jimmy, he introduced him to everyone. Jimmy connected pretty tightly with Pat because they had met each other at the recording studio with Bowie. Pat was there with his wife, Peggy, and the four of us really hit it off. In fact, we had dinner at Pat and Peggy's beautiful prewar apartment on Seventy-Second Street. I introduced our go-go dancer, Ellen, to Peggy, as she was looking for a job and Peggy was starting a catering business. I remember the three of us girls hanging in Peggy's kitchen with a bottle of red wine and gossip on our lips: a rare girly moment for me.

That night at Hurrah, though, Jimmy and Robert and Pat disappeared into Robert's office behind the bar. Jimmy didn't ask me to join them, because he knew I didn't want to be involved with drugs anymore. I decided

---

2   David says, "I don't think Jimmy came up with the 'ahhh looks . . .' but I know he had the idea for everyone to sing them together . . . including him. I can still hear the Brooklyn accent if I listen hard."

to stay at the bar and watch Suicide. Ellen was there, and as we gabbed, I asked the bartender for another ginger ale. Then I went to the bathroom, but when I came out and was heading back to the bar, I started to feel really drunk. I almost fell over. Except I hadn't had any liquor. When I finally got back to my barstool and sat down, the drunk feeling disappeared and I felt better. I quietly looked around me. Then, suddenly, the room broke distinctly in two. Ellen came over and started talking again, and when I looked at her, she was double—two Ellens. I looked at the band on the stage. They were double, too—two Suicides. It was back. But I had stopped the drugs. I had stopped the alcohol. However, the double vision was back.

The next day when I woke up, I immediately sat up in bed. I felt great. Strong. Rested. Refreshed. But everything was still double. Everywhere I turned, my eyes saw double. I went to the bathroom and looked at myself. Double. Two of me. Putting on my makeup was a trial, to say the least, and the odd thing was, I felt great. I wasn't tired or dizzy at all. Just, the world . . . was all in double.

I got some orange juice out of the fridge. Jimmy was still asleep upstairs. Suddenly, the phone rang.

"You're going to be on time, right?"

It was Philip.

"For the gig tonight? Of course, what are you talking about?" I asked.

"Well, you've missed two rehearsals, and the Squat sound check. And . . ." He paused.

"And what?" I asked.

"You're not around anymore."

"Sure I am," I said. "I'm right here."

I rubbed my eyes. Still double.

"Here," he said. "With us. You're not with us."

"That is so not true, Philip." I looked at my watch. "I'll meet you at the show," I said. "Antone has the equipment?"

"Yeah," he said. "Don't be late." And he hung up.

I looked around the room. Double. It didn't seem like it might waver or disappear. It was here to stay. But I felt really good. And even though everything was in double, I still could see. I could manage anything. Jimmy creaked down the stairs and asked for some coffee. I quickly made it for him and thought about Town Hall. I was sure I could play the gig that night. I was sure of it.

• ● •

THE TOWN HALL GIG WAS WITH THE KNOW and Rob Tyner and the MC5. It was a huge theater. There were more than a thousand seats, although, only about three hundred were filled for our show. Luckily, MB met me there. It wasn't that I needed help with anything, but I felt better that she was there with me. She was also the first one I told about my vision. And by that point, it was getting hard to hide it. My left eye had become fixed in the center. It wasn't moving. MB looked at it while we were in the bathroom.

"You can see?" she asked.

"Yeah. Just, it's all double." I said.

"It looks weird," she remarked.

I pushed past her and gazed at my left eye in the mirror. It stared straight ahead. When I moved my eyeballs, my right eyeball turned, but my left eyeball didn't. It just stayed there.

"I can see, though. I can do stuff," I said.

"You can play?" MB asked.

"Sure!"

A woman came in and went to a stall at the end.

"It's kind of obvious," MB said. "When you look at it, you can see it."

I turned back around to the mirror and looked again.

"Yeah," I said. "Fuck."

About an hour later, the show was about to start and we went onstage before the curtain rose, for a quick prep. I was careful to keep my face hidden so no one would see my freaky frozen eye as I swiftly adjusted the drums. In fact, most of the time I either stayed in the bathroom with MB or in a small room off the side of the dressing room. Luckily, Jimmy was hanging out front by the crowd because Clem, Blondie's drummer, was there to see the Know.

When we finally jumped onstage, we got a terrific response from the audience. It was a big venue, but we were getting used to that. I jumped behind the drums, trying to keep my head down, although because I was in the back, it was unlikely that anyone could see my face very clearly, let alone my left eye. Being in the back has its advantages.

Our first song was "Christmas Weather," and after everyone had plugged into their amps and checked their levels, David looked at Bill, who started the first notes, and we launched into the pounding beginning. This was true metronome work on my part, and I heard Jimmy scream for us after we started.

It was in no way a difficult beat to play—simple, steady—a background pulse to carry the song.

Except I wasn't keeping up.

I barely got through "Christmas Weather" and then "Channel 13," but after the third song, "Roof Party," I started really falling behind, and not just by a few beats. It was noticeable.

It wasn't that I couldn't see the drums. Despite my double vision, I could visually perceive everything around me just fine. The problem was that I was having trouble lifting the drumsticks. The muscles in my arms started feeling heavy, and lifting the sticks fast enough to keep up with everyone else became nearly impossible. After my miserable performance on "Roof Party," everyone rushed over.

"What's happening?" David asked. "Are you okay?"

"Yeah—are you stoned?" Philip added."

"No!" I said. "I don't know what's happening."

I tried to not lift my face much. I didn't want them to see my eye. Just then, Jimmy jumped onto the stage with Clem.

"Guys, you sounded like shit out there. Laura, what's going on?" he asked.

"I don't know! I don't know!" I screamed.

"Why don't you let Clem take the rest of the set, okay?" he suggested.

Some people in the audience screamed, wanting to know what was happening. I got up, handed Clem my sticks, and thanked him. I dashed off the stage and ran to the small room next to the dressing room. Tears streamed out of my eyes. MB ran in and hugged me. Then Jimmy came in.

"What the hell is going on?"

I lifted my head and looked at him—with both eyes. My frozen left eye quivered.

"Shit!" he shrieked.

. ● .

TWO DAYS LATER, I WAS LYING IN BED staring at the ceiling. It was still double. A broken, distorted white ceiling, slanting into itself. I turned my head and looked at the alarm clock. It was 9:30 a.m.—or 9:30-ish, in sideways world.

I shifted my head back. Jimmy wasn't there. I sat up. The entire room was double. Two—or partial two—of everything. It wasn't moving, though, so I figured it would be easy to navigate.

I looked back at Jimmy's spot. I guessed he was out with Joey Wilson preparing production of Wilson's album.[3] He would be gone for the next twenty-four hours, no doubt. I actually thought that he might be staying away because the whole thing with my vision was weird; it was too much. I'm not sure if that's what was happening with him. But it wouldn't surprise me. I was a little unnerved by it all myself.

Thing was, I could see fine—just double. And my energy was fine and everything else was fine. I decided this all would pass.

Just then, the phone rang.

"Hello?"

"Hi, it's me."

"Philip? Hey! What's up?" I asked.

"We need to talk," he said. "Can we come over?"

"Uh, sure—wait, who's we?"

"All of us," he said.

"The band?"

"Yeah," he said.

That was strange. It was rare for all of them to come over at one time. In fact, that hadn't happened since Jimmy and I had moved here, six months previously.

"When did you want to come by?" I asked. I looked at the clock.

"Actually, we're around the corner."

A few minutes later, the doorbell rang. I jumped into my jeans and T-shirt and grabbed my Ray-Bans and put them on. I hadn't shown them my frozen eyeball yet.

I ran downstairs.

---

3   Joey Wilson was a new wave singer from Philadelphia. His first album, produced by Jimmy, is called *Going Up*.

When I opened the door, they all filed in methodically, a battalion of soldiers marching back from battle, broken and exhausted, now returning to report on the state of the war.

Philip went to the refrigerator and got some orange juice. David and I sat down at the table while Bill, Lori, Joe, and Jody all sank into the couch.

"Where's Antone?" I asked. It seemed like this was a full meeting, so I figured we should all be here, although I wasn't sure why.

"He had to work," Jody piped in.

David offered me a Marlboro.

"Want one?"

I shook my head. He lit one up as Philip wandered over and sat down.

I looked around, and everyone was oddly silent. It had never been like this before. We were always right on with each other—gossiping, digging at each other, laughing and poking—a tight group.

But at that point, everyone seemed to be in another dimension—and I felt like the disease in the room. I turned to Philip.

"What's going on?"

"We want you out of the band," he said.

"What!?"

My mouth dropped open. I couldn't find air. The skin on my body prickled. It felt like the walls were coming down on me.

I was shocked.

"It's not working anymore," David said, blowing his words out through his smoke.

"What's not working? Me? You mean Town Hall?" I asked. "Look," I pleaded, "that was nothing! It was just something that happened," I insisted.

I rubbed my cheeks, then my eyes, then behind my ears, then my neck. I wasn't even itchy. I don't know what I was.

Then I remembered my frozen eye. I looked at David and Philip and turned to the others. No one spoke. The stagnation in the room stopped the ticking of the phantom clock. For that moment, time between all of us was stock-still.

"Okay, I've been overdoing it," I quietly said. "Too much coke. Too much booze. But I'm done with that."

"That's not it, Laura," Philip said.

"What, then—what is it?" I begged.

"You keep bailing out!" he yelled. "You keep missing rehearsals! You didn't even show up for the sound check at Squat! Jesus!"

He stood up and seemed to implore the others to stand, but no one budged.

"Yes, Town Hall was a problem and Squat was a problem, but it's not that," David interjected. "You're not a part of us anymore, Laura," he continued. "You're not in our world anymore."

"Of course I am!" I shrieked. "I'm the drummer!"

"And you've gotten a little bossy," Philip squeaked. "You've changed."

I looked over at Bill. He was sitting at the far end of the sofa, near the window—probably so he could escape quickly.

"Bill?" I meekly said to him.

He dropped his head down as I turned my eyes to him. I thought back to when I'd first talked to him at Friends. It had been in Mr. Schwartz's class on Chaucer. Bill was sitting at the far back desk, in the corner. There were three empty desks around him. I was new and nervous, but I sat down near him and smiled. The rest of the class stayed away from us. We were the impurity in the corner, to be avoided.

I remember he was reading the *Village Voice*'s listings of bands playing at the clubs. I was skittish, but I leaned over the paper and asked what he was looking at. That was the beginning, for me, and it was a million years ago. My best friend. I kept thinking about it all. How had all this happened—and so fast?

I looked at Lori. She looked back at me, then turned away. My dear old friend. How did I lose her? And Jody. She had saved me over and over. She even let me crash at her tiny Lower East Side apartment after a blowout with Jimmy. The place barely had room for her and her bed, but she took me in anyway.

David and Philip stood up.

"You're in a different world and it's not with us. You're with the Blondies and Bowie and jetting everywhere. You're not here, with us. In body, yes, when you care to show up. But your heart is gone," David said.[4]

---

4 David's memory: "I remember somehow summoning the courage and deciding to be the one to deliver the 'final word' on the subject. I loved you and hated saying it, but thought it wouldn't happen if I didn't actually say it. We brought booze for fortitude and I took a gulp and dropped the axe. I can't remember the exact words. But after I said it, so did everyone else, in their way. You went upstairs and called Jimmy and said, 'I'm not a Student Teacher anymore!' and were very upset. Crying. It was traumatic all around I think. I know I was wrecked."

Me with Chris, Debbie, and Jimmy. (Seated woman unknown.)
(PHOTO BY ROBERTA BAYLEY)

The girl in the back.
(AUTHOR'S COLLECTION)

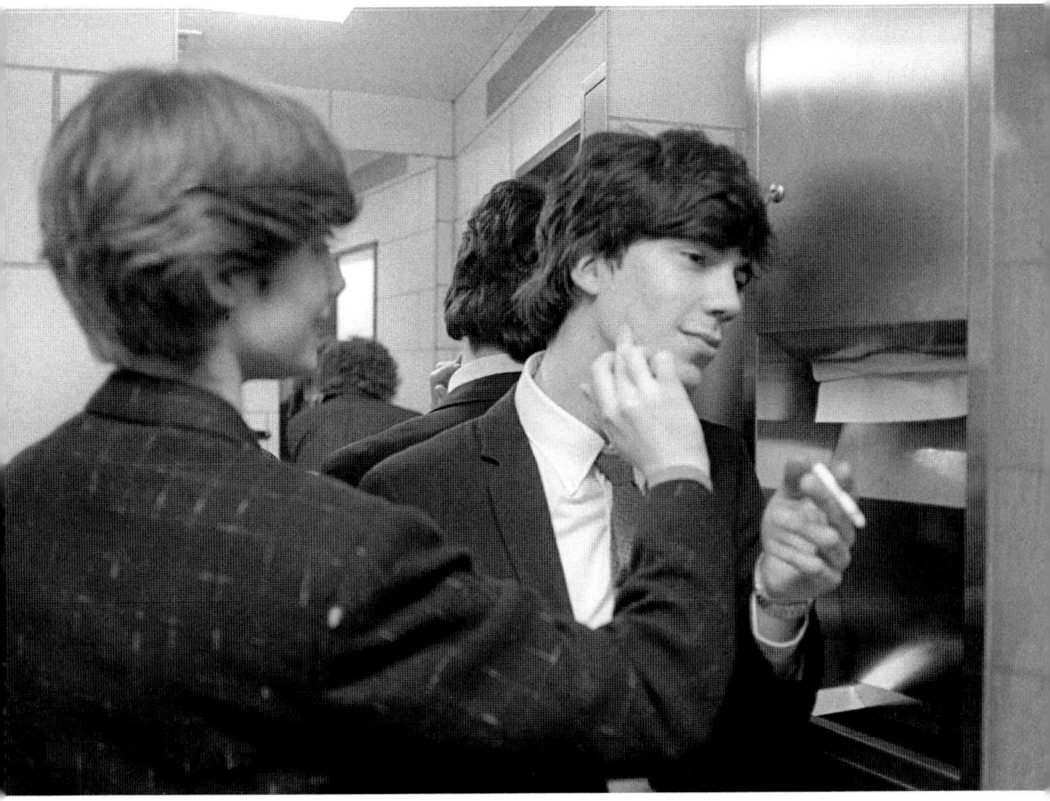

Helping Jimmy
with his makeup.
(PHOTO BY
ROBERTA BAYLEY)

Doing the best I can.
(AUTHOR'S COLLECTION)

L.K Scotland 1979

Scotland, 1979.
(AUTHOR'S COLLECTION)

From a Student Teachers photo session.
(PHOTO BY STEVE LOMBARDI)

Jimmy and me after one of my gigs. (AUTHOR'S COLLECTION)

For modeling portfolio.
(AUTHOR'S COLLECTION)

Ignorance is bliss.
(PHOTO BY
JOE STEVENS)

Jimmy and me,
young and hopeful.
(PHOTO BY
JOE STEVENS)

They went to the door and everyone followed. David opened it to leave, and they all filed out. Bill turned and gave a small, sad wave as he followed the rest of them. Philip was the last to go and he turned back to me. I saw, in his face, the boy I knew when the band started, back at Doug's loft. It had been ten lifetimes since then for both of us. I'd loved him then. I still loved him. He was—they all were—my family. What had I done? What was happening?

"I'm not a Student Teacher anymore," I said, tears filling my eyes.

"I'm sorry," Philip said, and he turned away.

All I could think, as I heard them walk down the hall, was that I was the one who should be apologizing.

27

11:59

A FEW DAYS AFTER THE BAND LEFT, I DEVELOPED A SORE on the left side of my tongue, which I basically ignored. Then, two weeks after that, the double vision hadn't stopped. I knew that doing too much coke could badly affect your mouth, and well, everything really—but I had stopped it for a few weeks already, almost a month. I had been sure all the septicity eating my eye and my tongue would disappear.

It didn't.

Early one morning, I got out of bed and went downstairs to the bathroom and stuck my tongue out at the mirror. The sore had exploded up and down the entire left side. It was white and bulbous and gross, making it difficult to eat, drink, and even talk.

Why wasn't it all gone? I had stopped everything—the drugs, the booze, the crazy late hours—these weird things should all be gone.

I called my dad.

"I'm not feeling good, Dad," I said.

"What's wrong?" he asked.

"Something's wrong with my eye." I didn't bring up my tongue. I needed to keep this under control with him. I paused.

"I'm seeing double," I said.

"Can you see at all?" he asked.

"Yeah, Yeah! I see fine . . . it's just . . . all double."

For a moment, he didn't say anything, like he was involved in something more pressing.

"All right, go see Dr. Zimmerman. Jane will make an appointment for you."

"Okay," I said. I didn't want this. Any of it, I thought, as I hung up.

Dr. Zimmerman had been our family doctor since I'd come to New York. His daughter was even in my class at Friends. He was diminutive, with tight round eyeglasses and a big heart.

Jane called me back a few minutes later and said Dr. Zimmerman wanted to see me immediately. That was fast.

When I got to his office and told the receptionist I was there, he appeared at the door and waved me in.

I sat down and he quickly checked my eye, running his fingers across my line of sight, and then asked to see my tongue. I hadn't even mentioned my tongue to him.

"Get to the hospital. I want you to see Dr. Abraham Lieberman," he commanded. Then he turned and started dialing the phone.

"What? Who's that?" I asked.

"A neurologist," he said. He called my dad and Jane, and a few minutes later, Jane and MB picked me up at Zimmerman's office in a taxi.

Dr. Lieberman's office was at New York University Hospital. He was elfin, with graying skin and a limp from a bout with polio he'd endured as a kid. The sick examining the sick, I thought to myself.

He was also Muhammad Ali's doctor and made sure everyone knew that the minute they entered his office. There were pictures of him with Cassius Clay everywhere. He was nice enough, although with a slight air of self-importance. But then it occurred to me, when I looked at him, as he asked me to follow his moving finger with my eyes and to squeeze his hand as hard as I could, while he leaned on his cane—what did "sick" mean anyway? The examination took a total of sixty seconds; then he ordered me into the hospital to get a CAT scan.

MB and Jane were with me as they rolled me into the CAT scan and then to my room. I was getting more and more tired, the deeper those doctors pushed me into whatever this was. I ended up in the juvenile ward but I didn't know why, I had been eighteen years old for four months already. And it was annoying, because the kids on the floor cried a lot, and at all hours. Although I didn't blame them. I didn't want to be there either.

Meanwhile, Jimmy wasn't around. He was still at Chelsea Recording Studios with Joey Wilson. A hospital was the last place he'd be. I called him that first night and he sounded good, though not talkative. It was a confused episode for both of us. Neither of us had an inkling as to why I was in the hospital but, even more significantly, we were living in an alternate world where nothing had a negative impact on us whatsoever.

That unspoken feeling of being invulnerable wasn't drug-fueled: It was a fact of our life. Jimmy often talked about the bubble he lived in as a rock star, and the truism of that kind of life—when you're in that sphere of wealth and fame, you're untouchable. After a little while of living in that state, the slick silver shield against the real-world sufferings becomes a part of your skin, more than second nature—it's all you know. So Jimmy not being at the hospital was no big deal.

He did end up visiting me, bringing flowers and a two-foot-tall teddy bear. He declared his endless love for me and said he felt terrible being so tied up with the production work, but after he left, I knew it was better for him to stay away. He couldn't handle the hospital very well. Being there didn't make any sense to him. It wasn't a reality that was genuine, inside the bubble, and it was okay that he wasn't there with me. To him, I could've been out of town visiting my mom or friends.

Except I wasn't.

Today could last a million years.[1]

I stayed in that hospital room for the next two weeks. No one told me to do anything except to rest and "take these pills here." A few days after I got there, the nurses dragged me to a big metallic washroom down the hall for a bath, where I had the humiliating and demeaning experience of them washing my naked body as I lay flat on a gurney. Why I couldn't just get off the gurney and take my own shower, I don't know.

At the end of the first week, I got a call from Debbie. She and Chris had just moved into a town house mansion and she was having trouble adjusting to the huge space. Her voice even echoed on the phone, as she talked. But she was so sweet, even through the echoing words.

---

1 "11:59" by Jimmy Destri from Blondie's *Parallel Lines*, 1978.

Five days after I was admitted and had begun taking the medication, the nurse woke me to take my 6 a.m. pill, and as I pushed myself up and lifted my eyelids to see her, I was stunned. There was only one of her. Not two. I swung my head around. It was all one—all the way it should be. It had been five weeks since my vision had gone haywire, and now I was seeing everything the right way. I smiled and took my pill, but I couldn't get back to sleep. I was too happy.

Eventually, after I had been stuck inside that prison cell/hospital room for about twelve days, Dr. Lieberman finally came in. He was followed by five interns and two nurses. I couldn't imagine that whatever he had to tell me required him to bring so many bodies with him. He sat down on the bed and told me I had multiple sclerosis.

"What?" I asked.

"It's a neurological condition" he said.

I had no idea what he was talking about.

"There's no cure at the moment, but there's no doubt in my mind there will be one in about ten years," he said. "When you're, what . . ." He looked at my chart. "When you're twenty-eight!" he said and beamed, tapping my leg.

He then told me he was putting me on a two-week course of steroids but that I could go home and take them, as long as I rested, stayed in bed, and gave my body time to recover. Apparently, I had been through an exacerbation of the condition and I needed time to recuperate.

After he left, I immediately called my mom, but she wasn't home, so I called my dad.

"Yes, I heard," he said.

"You heard?" I was incredulous. "And you didn't tell me?"

"The doctor wanted to tell you. But Zimmerman said it's a mild form, Laura. You'll be fine," he said.

I paused. My left thumb trembled. I pushed it under my thigh.

"You're sure I'll be okay?"

"Absolutely," he said.

28

LUKE AND LAURA

I WAS VERY WORRIED ABOUT HER.

"What if Hutch finds them and kills her? What is Luke going to do without her?" I asked.

MB handed me a bowl of peanuts.

"He'll get over it," she said, kicking her feet up onto the ottoman. "Luke can totally take care of himself. He's a gangster, for chrissakes!"

I was stationed on the floor, in the living room of Jimmy's and my apartment, recuperating on the mattress from our bed. We had moved it down there so I wouldn't be holed up in the loft room upstairs, away from life. MB was spending most of her time with me, which was helpful because Jimmy was gone all the time at the studio. The week after I got home, my mom came up to New York. She ended up staying at the Drake Hotel but spending all her time with me.

One night, she was over at the apartment, making my favorite dinner of roast turkey and mashed potatoes. In the end, I was a true-blue Southern girl, and to prove it, MB and I watched the invincible J. R. Ewing on *Dallas* while Mom basted the turkey.

As J. R. fought with Cliff, Jimmy walked in the front door with Bowie in tow. I immediately sat up on the mattress and brushed back my hair. I looked like shit.

"Hey, everyone! Look who's here!"

Mom edged out of the kitchen, wiping her hands on a towel.

"David, this is Laura's mom," Jimmy said.

Bowie reached his hand out to her.

"Virginia," Mom said, introducing herself.

They shook.

"Good to meet you. David," Bowie replied.

My mom lit up. She followed him into the living room. I got up off of the mattress. I was still feeling shaky. It may have been because of the steroids, or because I wasn't moving around enough. Or both. But my eye was back to normal, at least.

Bowie gave me a tight, affectionate hug. Jimmy stood behind him, downing a beer and smiling.

"How are you?" he asked.

"Fine."

"So what are the doctors saying?" Bowie asked.

"Um, what is it . . . Oh, it's multiple sclerosis, they said. I don't know much about it," I told him.

Bowie pulled me close to him again. Did he know about it? I wondered to myself. After a few minutes, Mom put out a full dinner on the table and Jimmy urged Bowie to sit down. MB joined them, but I stayed on my mattress. The steroids were still eating into me.

Dinner ended up lasting over two hours, and Bowie spent most of the time talking to my mom about her work at the National Academy of Sciences in DC and his visit to Japan the previous month. They were two hens in the laundry room, gabbing about their annoying kids and the abusive cost of milk at the supermarket.

After they had coffee, my mom asked Bowie what he thought I should do now. I wanted to strangle her, but the hens had become fast friends.

"I think she should go into modeling," Mom announced.

I dropped back on the mattress and covered my face with a magazine. Luckily, Jimmy stepped in.

"Actually, we need to get back to the studio now," he said. Thank God, I thought.

He gave me a kiss and said he'd be home later. Bowie gave my mom and MB a goodbye, then came over to me on the mattress.

"When do you think you'll be back?" he asked, his eyes alone holding me up.

"Soon," I said. "Very soon."

"Great!" he said, and hugged me again. Then he and Jimmy went out the front door and I lay back down and turned over. I grabbed the stuffed owl that Jimmy had given me when we were in Germany last year. I think he gave it to me because he knew I adored the King Arthur legend, especially Merlin's trusty, shrewd owl, Archimedes.

I surrounded Archimedes with my arms and looked out the living room window, questioning whether I would be able to hang out with Bowie again, or play the drums again, or do anything.

· ● ·

A FEW WEEKS LATER, because the recording Jimmy had been doing with Wilson was finished, he decided to take a brief break before he went into final production work. Robert Boykin had planned to rent a cottage at the beach in Amagansett on Long Island and asked if we wanted to join him. I was still taking steroids, so a peaceful vacation at the beach sounded perfect.

The cottage was situated down the street from Pat and Peggy Gibbons' house. We had become closer with them as Jimmy worked more with Bowie, and the Gibbonses usually vacationed in the summers in Amagansett. Along with Robert, Marc and Ellen came with us. I still needed rest and calm, and I truly wondered if that would be in the cards while we were out there.

The tip of Long Island, where Amagansett is located, along with the Hamptons and Montauk, is by far the best part of New York for one single reason: It's located way out in the middle of the Atlantic Ocean. It was as if the point of the island was really floating off, away from the coast. Whenever I was out there, not only did I always have a pure beachy experience, with sand inside the shells of the clams I ate at the local restaurant, but I could stand on the beach and dream about being sucked into the vast, tranquil mystery of the Atlantic.

It was the start of the summer season, so not all of the beach houses, lined along the oceanfront, were filled with people yet, but they were getting close. The portion of the island we were situated on was one of the farthest out, near the eastern point, and the town was checkered with fresh food stands and stores with beach umbrellas and surfboards bursting through the front doors.

The house we stayed in was a small three-bedroom beach cottage a few blocks back from the shore. After we arrived late on a Sunday night and collapsed into our beds, we awoke to a bright, shining cottage with an overwhelming sea scent pouring through the windows. I remember thinking that I could hear the waves so close to us, I was sure they were lapping at the walls of the cottage. I fantasized that we had actually been pulled underwater while we slept, into the darkened depths of the cool, safe ocean, and that everything here, on land, had all been a hallucination.

Within minutes of waking up, everyone grabbed an orange or a banana from the kitchen and headed to the beach. Jimmy put on his swimsuit and danced around the living room. He wanted me to come with him, but I was still feeling shaky from the steroids, so he went off without me. I sat in a lounge chair on the backyard deck, drinking an iced tea and reading *The Shining*. It felt so luxurious sitting in the quiet, under the sun. I turned on the cassette player next to me and listened to some Bob Marley. It was near heaven. I was feeling more rested, and I could feel myself getting stronger, back to my old self.

Later that night, we headed over to Pat and Peggy's place for a barbecue. They had a stunning triple-decker house with a huge balcony hanging over a pool in their backyard. There was champagne flowing everywhere and dishes of barbecued salmon and braised chicken, which Peggy passed around to all of us. She was experimenting with recipes for her catering business. The Stones album *Some Girls* was on the stereo, and everyone hung out on the back patio, eating and drinking and laughing. After dinner was finished, Jimmy pulled out his packets and laid twenty lines of coke out on the dinner table.

I had hoped this venture to the beach wouldn't go there—that maybe everyone would move away from the drugs and getting stoned. Yes, I was in a place now with my health where I couldn't do drugs anymore— nor did I even want to, and my fence-sitting self had foolishly hoped the beach air and the sun and surf might breathe something new into everyone, into Jimmy—but it didn't. Life was at a point then where there was no reality—at the beach, in the city, anywhere—without drugs.

Later, back at our cottage, I was in the bathroom, brushing my teeth, and I noticed the skin on my arm was all red and blotchy. I checked my other arm and then my chest. Everywhere was red and blotchy. What was going on? At that moment, Jimmy came in.

"Look at this," I said. He checked my arms and my back and my chest.

"You got too much sun," he said. "We'll get some aloe vera later. Come on, let's got to bed," he said, pulling my arm.

"But it shouldn't be red and blotchy like this. That's weird, don't you think?" I asked.

"Don't worry about it. It's nothing. Come on."

He pulled me again.

"Not now honey, I'm still getting over this whole thing and these steroids really suck," I said. "I need to take a shower." I reached for a towel under the sink.

"No," he suddenly said.

"What?"

"I'm tired of this!" he snapped. "You never want to have sex anymore!"

"Shhh!" I whispered heatedly. "There are other people in the house, Jimmy!"

Suddenly, he pulled my shorts off and grabbed my waist, then pulled down his pants and rammed me into the vanity, pushing my back so hard that my head hit the mirror and the edge of the vanity ripped into my back.

"What are you doing?" I cried.

He pushed my head into the mirror again. I started sobbing as he repeatedly slammed into me. After a moment, he stopped. He was panting. Sweat streamed down his face. He looked at me, my tears dripping onto his arm. Then he lifted his hand off my waist and I dropped down off the counter. As I slid down, the flesh on my back tore. I felt blood sliding down onto my butt. I gasped, then quickly stopped myself, trying hard to keep quiet.

After a moment, he opened the door, looked back at me, then left and shut it stiffly behind him. I sat down on the toilet. I reached into the shower and turned on the water but stayed sitting on the toilet. I gulped and coughed through more tears. I lifted my eyes and looked back at the door. Who was he? I didn't know what to think, or what to do.

After about a half hour, I washed my face and wiped the blood off my back. I grabbed another towel and quietly opened the bathroom door. I heard Ellen and Marc gabbing in the living room about going to a movie in East Hampton. I slipped around the door and into the bedroom and shut it. Jimmy was sitting on the bed with his head in his hands. I walked to the edge and sat down.

"I'm sorry," he said.

"I know," I replied.

He flopped back next to me and lay there looking up at me. I didn't look at him. I kept the towel close to my chest.

"I'm really stressed. Shit's going down with the band," he said, eyeing the ceiling.

"I know."

"It's the stress," he said, and leaned over and kissed my knee. "I'm sorry."

"I know," I said.

• ● •

THE FOLLOWING MONTH, BLONDIE TOOK OFF for Hollywood. They were scheduled to record *Autoamerican* at United Western Recorders, not far from the strip. They were doing the record with Mike Chapman, who had worked with them on *Parallel Lines*, which had really sent them hurtling into international success, and Chapman was a big part of that accomplishment.

During the first few weeks, we were set up in an apartment complex just outside of Hollywood. It was up in the hills. A stretch of three-story town houses built of hazy cedar and cement, it smacked of a hotel-apartment—big, melancholy rooms, indistinct colors, and a kitchen that was empty except for a coffeemaker. There was a TV in the corner of the living room, and a desolate fireplace. It was another stop on the temporary merry-go-round of hotel life on the road.

It had been about six weeks since I had been diagnosed and I was still sort of in recuperation mode, so I was resting a lot. I think I was in more of a state of suspension between what was and what could be. I even felt that way physically, as if I was walking on soft air everywhere, because nothing was solid, nothing was definite. No matter where I went, there was no clarity, only uncertainty.

The apartment complex was a busy place. Jimmy took off to the studio every day and I usually went out to the pool to rest and read. Despite the overwhelming feeling of transience of the place, of slipping time, of fleeting moments that expired and disappeared—when I looked around me, there were people living their lives: bustling families with their kids jumping into the pool, laughing and shrieking, with big smiles filled with glee. And there were plenty of single people roaming around, looking for a hookup.

It all felt very unreal. It was not just that I was floating between identities at that time, but there was a cultural difference. Not only did the streets and the buildings around Hollywood feel illusory, as if I was imagining it all, but the feeling was exacerbated by the cavernous suffocation of the studio where Blondie were recording.

Like most studios, United Western in downtown Hollywood had walls made of bleached-blonde wood, no windows, and artificial oxygen. What was even stranger to me was that when I walked outside of the studio there were no people. No one. There were sidewalks and streets and other buildings. But no life. Coming from New York City, where you couldn't cross the street without dodging fifty people, that nothingness, that street silence freaked me out. I've always had a problem with silence and any seeming emptiness. And those vacant streets made me tremble inside.

Whenever I joined Jimmy at the studio, I would sit in the waiting room watching the hundredth television hanging from the hundredth waiting room wall. That existence itself began wearing me down. Sometimes, to ward off the weight of it all, I watched Bruce talk on the phone, writing up notes in his book, which hung out of the briefcase on his lap. He was so busy and productive: The lack of air and light was inconsequential to him. It was the same for Debbie and Chris and Clem and Jimmy and Nigel and Frank—they were busy creating their project, their work. The suffocating fiction of the recording studio world had no effect on them— it was a means to an end. But it was starting to destroy me.

One of the worst parts of Hollywood was that the sun shone every day. There were never any clouds or rain. The second-worst part was that

I couldn't get anywhere unless I drove a car. I couldn't just walk around the corner to the deli and get a soda or some M&M's. I had to get in a car and drive somewhere to get those M&M's. It was very frustrating.

A bright spot, though, was Michael Des Barres. He was a friend of Nigel's because they'd been in a glam-rock band together back in England in the early '70s, called Silverhead. Always hot with red, penetrating energy, Michael was unique. He made me laugh whenever he was around. He and Jimmy became great friends and we went to his son's birthday party, where we met his wife at the time, Pamela Des Barres, and we went to a number of his shows promoting his album *I'm Only Human*.

After a few weeks, we moved into the Chateau Marmont and stayed in one of the cottages on the hotel's grounds. Debbie and Chris stayed in the cottage across from us, and this move was a godsend. We went from a bad B movie in the Hollywood Hills, stuck inside motley strips of a potential fake Hitchcock movie, to freedom and oxygen in downtown L.A.

The cottage was much smaller than the apartment we had been in, but there was no way of beating not only the remarkable history of the hotel but its beautiful and unique architecture. So many celebrities had stayed there, from Rock Hudson and Clark Gable to Mick Jagger and Robert Plant. The place just smelled of that kaleidoscopic celluloid world that we only ever see on the screen or in theaters. It was near intoxicating to wander through the gardens around the bungalows and experience the charm of the 1940s-style lobby, with its velvet armchairs and big lemon-shaded lamps. I even thought I might have seen Marlene Dietrich sitting in the corner, reading. Or I hoped.

Staying there during the rest of the recording provided a much-needed gust of respiration. Also, one of the songs Jimmy and I had worked on was being recorded at the studio, and that made me feel a bit more alive.

It was called "Angels on the Balcony." The most distinctive thing about the difference between "Angels" and "Slow Motion," which we worked on for Blondie's *Eat to the Beat* album, was the essence of the words. In "Slow Motion," we had put in words about the Student Teachers:

What's all that commotion that you hear?
The girl in the back who was doing the quake
Got a bellyache, she can't concentrate
Pick up the beat, you can move like you're made out of vapor

"Catch me if you can" is what she said with her hands
Come on and take me back (can you take her back?)[1]

When Jimmy and I had first started thinking about "Slow Motion" together, we were in the back of CBGB after one of the Student Teachers shows when I started talking to him about the idea of catching me if he could—that I would always be on the run. It was all in fun and he loved the line, so we took it back to his small recording synthesizer at the apartment and fleshed out the song. It was a process of collaborating between best friends, the one we loved.

But with "Angels on the Balcony," the words turned decidedly darker:

Silent light in the theater's sky
Phantom cigarette and a silent cry
The door swings open and it's cold outside
Run and hide, run and hide[2]

We would work on the song when Jimmy got back to the cottage, at the end of the recording day. But our discussion was often so distant, almost as if we were talking beyond each other, past one another, traveling different highways—and they weren't crossing one another, anywhere. There were no intersections.

It wasn't that working on "Angels" was a chore, it was just—nothing. Despite the romance of living in the Chateau Marmont, under the tent of Blondie's stratospheric success, neither of us seemed to feel any enthusiasm about coming up with the lyrics or building up the song. I don't know exactly why the emotion behind the lyrics changed, except, with the introduction of knowledge, time, and the loss of innocence, there is often an unfortunate erosion between two people.

About a week after Blondie had worked on "Angels" in the studio, Jimmy got a call from Greg Gorman. Greg was a high-powered celebrity photographer who had done a lot of work with rock 'n' roll icons, starting with Jimi Hendrix in 1968. Apparently, he wanted to help me put together

---

1 "Slow Motion" by Jimmy Destri and Laura Davis from Blondie's *Eat to the Beat*, 1979.

2 "Angels on the Balcony" by Jimmy Destri and Laura Davis from Blondie's *Autoamerican*, 1980.

a portfolio to get into modeling. Although Jimmy and I had discussed this possibility, I didn't think it would go anywhere and I wasn't sure I wanted it to. Plus, I certainly hadn't imagined starting with a heavyweight photographer like Greg Gorman.

The shoot was scheduled for the following morning. I was scared beyond words. This wasn't my world. I didn't know what to do with my hair or my makeup or what to wear, but Jimmy told me that Greg said all of that would be handled at his studio. That world was nowhere near my comprehension. I was a tomboy. I had always been a tomboy who had become a drummer. I didn't even own a dress. Being a model had never been on my short little list.

Modeling is an extremely difficult job, and I learned that the hard way. However, when we went to Greg's studio in West Hollywood, he made it a lot of fun.

"Don't move your eyelid," Greg's makeup artist instructed me.

I sat in his chair and fidgeted like mad. How could I not move my eyelid? That was impossible. "That's biology!" I screamed inside my head. Eyelids move!

Ah, the pretense . . . (PHOTO BY GREG GORMAN)

Greg's makeup artist was very patient with me, and after he finished, Jimmy and I did a photo shoot together. The studio was large and all white. Greg put on "Love Me Two Times," by the Doors, and Jimmy and I posed in very rock 'n' rolly, playful, mischievous ways. We also posed in more proper ways like a high-powered, well-known couple. I had a great time and it was a lot of fun and it made moving to a shoot of just me as the focus much easier. Throughout it all, however, Jimmy did coke with Greg and everyone else in the studio. I wondered if that was the payment.

The next day, in downtown Hollywood, Greg arranged a shoot where I stood against the granite wall of a building, and later turned and twirled near a fountain. Thing was, I had to wear a dress. I'd found a baby-blue T-shirt dress at a discount store for ten dollars. And I had to wear panty hose. Panty hose! Even worse, I had to wear white high heels. I thought I would explode, as my self-imposed control not to vomit threatened to break. But I had to do the shoot. Greg was doing it for free, and, even more significantly—I learned later—it had been set up by Bowie.

I don't know why he set up the photo session for me. Maybe it was because my mom had mentioned modeling as a possibility for me. It's not that I wanted to pursue it, and, honestly, I don't think Bowie thought it was the right avenue. It had nothing to do with the way I looked. Rather, it had to do with what I was, who I was—and modeling wasn't it.

• • •

TOWARD THE END OF THE SUMMER, as recording wrapped up, the long, steamy days at the cottage became draining. One afternoon, as I was heading out to meet my driving teacher—I had finally accepted that I had to learn how to drive, even though our stay in Hollywood was ending soon—I ran into Debbie, lying on a lounge chair in front, getting some sun.

"Hi, Debbie," I said as I walked toward the back gate. She turned her head to me.

"Oh, hey! Wait up!" she said and sat up. I stopped.

"How are you feeling?" she asked.

I walked over and sat on the stoop near her.

"Good. I feel, you know, like I always did. I mean, back to my old self really," I said. I hadn't even looked up what multiple sclerosis was since I'd left the hospital.

"Great," she said. "Come in, I have something for you."

I followed her into her cottage. Chris was laid out on the couch watching TV. I waved to him and he winked. Debbie went into the kitchen and came back with a plate with two slices of apple pie on it.

"I made a pie and it turns out there was too much, so I thought you guys would like some." She handed me the plate.

"Wow! Thanks. I didn't know you cooked."

"She does many things," Chris chimed in from the couch. Debbie ignored him and opened the front door.

"So we're leaving in a few days I guess," she said, as she sat back down on the chair outside.

"Yeah," I said. Then, as I went to put the pie slices in our cottage, Debbie stopped me.

"It's going to be okay, you know," she said, creasing her eyes under the blaring sunlight.

I looked at her, feeling I wanted to reassure her.

"I know," I said.

I couldn't imagine what could go wrong.

29

THE ELEPHANT MAN

THERE WAS ONE PROTEST HE MADE ALL OF THE TIME: that he was a man, not an animal. In 1862 in Leicester, England, Joseph Merrick was born with multiple abnormalities of his skin and skeleton. He grew into a life-size monster with an unrecognizable face. The flesh welling up from the side of his head became so large and heavy that he couldn't sleep lying down for fear of breaking his neck. Although he became a sideshow phenomenon and a medical mystery, his unique, and only, gift to history and the world was his grotesque look. That look was a fact, and it was how John Merrick was perceived, and that perception created his fame as well as his isolation.

In many ways, Bowie was perfect to play him. Both of them existed in ruinous isolation, created by the fame consuming both of their lives. Performing in *The Elephant Man* in the fall of 1980, Bowie embodied one of the most handsome men in the world living inside the body and mind of one of the ugliest men in history. We are all judged by how we look. Bowie knew that.

Jimmy and I got back from California in September, just days before we were to see Bowie on Broadway. While we were away, our friend John Browner had stayed at our apartment, and I expect it had been the center of many parties and love-ins. In fact, I heard Mick Jagger had been at the house to see John, and I remember interrogating him about where Jagger had actually stood and sat so I could memorialize those spots. I even considered putting gold ropes around the dining room chair and the end of the sofa where he had been, but was told no, that wouldn't be happening.

I felt physically fine and still didn't really know what multiple sclerosis was, nor had I made any effort to find out about it. No one had given me a pamphlet or a lecture about it when I was diagnosed six months earlier, so I didn't think about it. But what I did start thinking about was where I was and what was I going to do with myself.

After David and Philip had asked me to leave the band, the Student Teachers kept playing gigs and recording. They had brought in another female drummer named Hayden Brasseur, who had worked with Jimmy's sister, Donna. I heard in the wind that they were doing pretty well, but I had been away most of the time since I left the band, so I wasn't in touch with any of them. I had talked a little with Jody and Antone after the split, but not much.

I had come to realize that Philip was right. We had separated a long time before he and the band made it official. I thought about it for a long time while sitting at my table with my orange juice and egg sandwich while Jimmy was off doing production work. I had left the Student Teacher world without much thought, without much recognition, without even a thank-you. That was really terrible, because they were the beginning of everything in my world—from that moment when Bill gave me that big hug outside of Max's and we went inside to dance to the Mumps.

Jimmy was working on postproduction for the upcoming release of *Autoamerican*, and he was distracted with the plans for it. He also was continuing to do too much coke. He was up at all hours writing, playing his synthesizer, and recording. And he slept all day. I rarely saw him.

I went for a lot of walks alone around the neighborhood. My old gym teacher from eighth grade had opened a record store around the corner, and I often went in there, sifting through the record albums. I remember coming across one by a folk group called Wind in the Willows, in which Debbie had been a singer. I noticed that it was from 1968. Wow, I thought to myself, how different she had become—how different it all had become.

I was set to pursue modeling work with the portfolio Greg Gorman had put together. I found myself going to all the top modeling agencies— Elite, Ford, Wilhelmina—and sitting in the front lobby while some intern looked over my portfolio. Then, without fail, they came back out and told me I needed to lose five pounds, which really meant they needed more anorexia from me.

I usually did these rounds in the mornings, during the week. Then I would walk through Midtown and sit at outdoor cafés or on the lawn at Central Park, waiting for the day to reach 5 p.m. so I could go back home and pretend I had put in a profitable workday.

I didn't know what I was escaping, but for some reason, I was driven to go out and keep walking around.

The night we went to see Bowie on Broadway in *The Elephant Man*, we got dressed up for the first time in a long time. Even though I was pushing the modeling work, I still didn't own a dress, but I tried to look classy in my black jeans, black T-shirt, and white blazer. Boyish, tomboyish, but still okay, I thought. Jimmy looked very handsome in his suit. I remember watching him get dressed and missing him already. Even in the same room, he was somewhere else.

We had fourth-row seats at the Booth Theatre, and when we got there, it became very exciting. Although we had missed the opening week, the place was packed and charged up for this unique event.

When Bowie came out onstage, the audience went wild and the applause lasted a little longer than it should have. I could see him trying hard to maintain himself and his focus, waiting for the crowd to quiet. When they finally did, he launched into a remarkable portrayal, which I could see was physically and emotionally demanding, particularly since he had to maintain a distorted, slanted hold on his body for two hours. It looked grueling.

After the show, we met Bowie and Coco at a restaurant downtown on Varick Street, one block north of the Holland Tunnel. Although it was nearly 10:30 p.m., restaurants in New York City didn't usually close until past midnight. However, this restaurant was completely empty. I noticed, after we all filed in and sat down at the center table, that the waiter locked the front door of the restaurant and pulled black blinds down over the windows. I wondered if Vito Corleone would be joining us.

David and Coco sat next to Jimmy and me because we hadn't seen each other since Jimmy and I had left for California in June. Jimmy went on about the recording and the production challenges on *Autoamerican*. They had used an orchestra for the instrumental, "Europa"—a new experience that Jimmy really enjoyed. It was Mike Chapman's baby, but I sensed Jimmy wanted a piece of it.

We all worked through our first course and the waiter was refreshing drinks when Bowie got up, pulled his chair over, and sat down next to me.

"We haven't said hello," he said. My heart started exploding in small, silent eruptions.

"Well, you've been busy and, my God, great performance tonight," I said, trying desperately to remain composed.

"Thanks," he said. "What I want to know is, how are you doing?"

"Oh . . . uh . . . I'm fine. I feel great!" I said, trying to keep it very tight.

"Did you ever find out more about the disease?" he asked.

"No," I said. "But I will . . . uh . . . I plan to."

He smiled.

"How's the modeling going?"

"Well, they want that near-death look, and I'm having a hard time getting there." I giggled. "Thank you for the setup with Greg, by the way. I really appreciated that," I said.

He crossed his legs.

"You really shouldn't be doing this," he said. And his voice dropped a little, his tone becoming more serious. He took a sip of wine.

"Uh, no?" I asked.

"You know why?" he said.

I wondered if it was because I didn't have the right "look." The agent at Wilhelmina said I would make a lovely "junior" model because I was only five foot nine—small for high-fashion modeling—and I guess my lips weren't fat enough. She also said I had to lose another five pounds. Where was that five pounds that they all kept seeing located?

Bowie leaned back and looked at me carefully.

"Because you don't want to," he said. Then he moved closer and grabbed my hand. "Right?"

I thought for a moment.

"Listen to yourself," he urged. I looked at him.

"Listen."

I wondered if he could ever look disheveled, like after not showering for two days—if he could ever not look so beautiful. He was dressed in a pure white blouse and brown pants. His amber-blonde hair fell back into the air. Simple. Quiet. Handsome.

"What do you want to do?" he asked.

I thought more specifically; then I breathed deeply.

"Go to college," I said. He smiled.

"Then do that! Go to college. You don't need to be here. You don't need to be in rock 'n' roll. Follow yourself," he said.

I raised my glass to him and smiled back. I took another deep breath. And in that moment, and perhaps for the first time, I experienced a sense of relief that was complete and total. My gut and my lungs completely released. I could follow my heart.

"Hey, David! Do you have your car here?" shouted Jimmy as he stood up. Bowie told him that he did, and Jimmy grabbed the half-full bottle of wine on the table.

"Let's go to the Mudd Club!"

Everybody grabbed their coats and bags as the waiter opened the front door. When Bowie threw on his coat, Coco grabbed him and whispered something in his ear. I don't know what it was, but I noticed Coco didn't join us as we went downtown, which was unusual.

We spent the next three hours at the club, mostly talking, drinking, and doing drugs. Jimmy had a ball with David and a mass of hangers-on. I hung by the bar talking with Ellen and looking at my watch.

By the time we left, it was near 5 a.m. We took David's car back to our apartment first, but as we got out of the car, David followed us. I looked at him. He was really drunk and just wanted to lie down. He leaned on Jimmy as I waved the driver off, and when we got in the apartment, Jimmy guided David to the sofa, where he collapsed. I ran upstairs and got a blanket, then went to the sofa and covered him. Jimmy went upstairs to sleep, and I went to the bathroom to wash up.

A few minutes later, I came out drying my face. Cold, early sunlight strained through the window blinds. I'd turned and started toward the stairs when I heard something.

"Are you going to bed now?" Bowie whispered from the couch. His eyes were closed as he spoke. He was really tired.

I walked over and adjusted his blanket.

"Yes," I said quietly. I started to turn away.

"Wait," he said.

I bent down and kneeled on the floor next to him.

"I have a matinee tomorrow."

"I know," I said. "I'll set the alarm."

"Stay here. With me." He turned on his side, facing me. He opened his eyes and put his hand on the back of my neck and pulled me to him. We kissed for a moment, sweet and deeply. I put my arm around him and placed my face in his neck.

During that moment, I thought about when I'd first seen him in '76 at the Garden, how distant he'd been, how he was a moving ancient sculpture on that monolithic stage, never to be touched, never to be known. Not human. Never human.

I lifted my head and watched him. Silent. In the stillness of the half-darkened room, his face was at once alive and motionless. I could see a moment to paint him, to sketch and capture that instant of boundless elegance. If I only could.

He was still half-awake, but sleep was quickly taking him. He looked exquisite. I was still breathing, but barely—being so near him, it was like his beauty hurt my heart. It was so hard to let go of him.

And even after all that time knowing him, I still felt, inside my bones, some otherworldly force had been at work in determining not only that I actually got to meet him, but that I got to know him, talk to him about more than rock 'n' roll, introduce him to my mother, even. But the reality was, as I felt his chest lift under my head with each breath, that I was probably wrong. That he was human. Though not entirely.

. • .

THE NEXT DAY, I WOKE UP AND FRANTICALLY looked at the alarm clock. It was 4:30 p.m. Damn! Bowie's matinee! I pushed Jimmy awake, threw on my clothes, and raced downstairs. Bowie was still passed out on the couch. I turned the light on over the dining room table and quietly went to wake him up. I was a little worried about what a freaked-out David Bowie would be like so I nudged him gently.

"David? David?" I said. His eyes squeaked open and he looked up at me. Then he noticed the darkening late afternoon out the window. He sat up.

"What time is it?" he asked.

"Four thirty," I said.

He stood up quickly.

"Can I use your phone?" I pointed him to the phone on the dining room table and he quickly made a call. To Coco, I assumed. After a minute, he hung up.

"I have to go," he said, a little panicked.

Yes, I figured he did. I got his jacket and handed it to him.

"Would you take me to a cab?" he asked.

"Sure," I said and threw on a sweatshirt. Jimmy had gone back upstairs, still wiped out. David and I quickly left to find a taxi.

Outside, the dusk was dropping down all around us. My sweatshirt wasn't enough against the sharp September chill. I held my arms around me, looking everywhere for a cab. I wanted to get him into one as soon as possible. David generally avoided walking around outside, but he seemed very blasé about it as we moved forward.

"I'm dying for something to drink," he suddenly said. I looked at him nervously. Really? Now?

"Uh, okay," I said. "There's a deli right around the corner."

As we went into the deli, my anxiety level tripled and I wondered why he wanted to take this risk. A small store filled with people. Maybe he was really thirsty.

I told him to wait by the door and keep his head down. I raced to the back and got him a small orange juice. When I got back to the front and started to pay, he asked me to get a pack of cigarettes, which I did, and paid as quickly as I could. I handed him the juice and pushed him out the front door. I think he was a little hungover, because ever since I'd met him, he had always been strict and firm about avoiding crowds and staying hidden. But then I realized that all of those times, Coco had been with him—and she wasn't there then.

We turned out of the deli and as I tried to hurry to the corner, Bowie leisurely drank his juice and lit a cigarette. We were at Sixth Avenue, and there was an army of taxis swinging by. I swiftly hailed one and opened the door for him.

"You better get going," I said. I looked around, praying no one noticed him.

David got in and shut the door. I started to back away and lift my hand to wave but he reached out of the open window and grabbed it.

"Thank you," he said.

I smiled.

"Anytime," I said. I started to pull away but he stopped me again.

"Good luck," he said.

I looked into his eyes. He was still waking up.

"Thank you," I said. My heart twisted around twice.

It wasn't just that I had fallen in love with him. Everyone fell in love with him. Rather, it was a love evolving into an acceptance that he was human, with human failings, and that I felt, more than anything, pure and bottomless respect for him. I stood there for that moment, that swift, airtight, flashing moment, loving him in that way, that way he would never know about.

As the taxi took off, I watched him through the back window and thought again about that otherworldly portal that I was still convinced granted me the chance to know the man I adored and idolized. Although I had learned, in the previous few years, that despite all of the glamour and lights and money and fame, there is no otherworld where those famous creatures reside. They need to eat, sleep, have sex and families; they gain great things and lose great things. Like all of us. But I still wondered.

Whether it was actually that force or not, I'll never know. But once that taxi disappeared up Sixth Avenue, that ethereal portal closed for good. I never saw him again.

PART 3

30

THREE YEARS EARLIER

THE CROWD STUMBLED TO A QUIET as we dashed off the stage. The lights dimmed. Our fans screamed passionately for us—endlessly. They knew this was big for us. They were proud. As we went past the curtain, Jody handed each of us a towel and Antone guided us upstairs through the murky backstage to our dressing room as the audience chanted: "Iggy! Iggy!"

When we rolled into it, we all sat down and grabbed water and soda. Philip landed on the counter and heaved a huge sigh. I looked at him. I know he thought we blew it out there. He guzzled a beer as Lori grabbed her cigarettes and slipped next to him. She agreed. Bill and David were spinning through the entire room. Bill was still coming down from those high landings we had been on a few minutes before. David was sweating torrents and pacing around as he drank from a gallon jug of water.

Parents started roaming in and hugging and kissing and congratulating us. MB was there with Jimmy, who gave me a big kiss. He was thrilled and offered me a Budweiser. MB stuck close, which I loved. She kept me safe. I was cracking, a little unhinged in the moment. We had a lot of trouble out there. We had all struggled and really tried.

A moment later my father walked in with Jane and a bouquet of roses. I was dazed. Flowers?

"Well done," he said, bowing to me with his small affection. He handed me the bouquet, then Jane ran over and gave me a big hug.

"Thanks," I said.

"What's next? Madison Square Garden?" Dad snickered through the side of his mouth.

I laughed—a weak stooge laugh, not meaning anything.

"Well, we're heading to the Irish pub across the street, so we'd better get going," Dad said. "I'm meeting a colleague there."

"Oh, okay—well, have a good time," I said as he and Jane quickly went out. MB looked at me and took the flowers.

Jimmy decided he wanted to take us all to the Mudd Club to celebrate. After we all said our goodbyes to our moms and dads, everyone followed Jimmy to a limo waiting downstairs. I trailed behind them and stepped down the back stairs. When I got to the stage landing, I saw the Cramps playing onstage. They sounded great. They were tight and they were on. Professional.

That was the big time and we knew it. It felt immense to all of us. The thought lingering inside most of our heads wasn't whether we were up to it—we had already fallen off that cliff—but rather, would we be up to it in the future?

The next evening, Bowie came by our apartment with Coco to hang out and see how the show went. He wasn't able to make it because of a prior commitment. David and Philip were there, and the three of us lamented over how the stage speakers had sucked as we all listened to Michael Jackson's album *Off the Wall* and drank beer and Rémy Martin. Bowie was as animated as ever, going on about the demise of the music world, about politics, the philosophy of Kierkegaard and Nietzsche—a world of ideas flew out of him. It was a small, special moment.

A little while after Bowie lambasted the threats to the artist in society and Michael Jackson finished singing "Rock with You," the phone rang. Jimmy answered it. It was Nancy Jeffries from RCA. She had seen a number of our shows and wanted to sign us. Jimmy's gaze shot excitedly to me, then to Bowie.

"RCA wants to sign the Student Teachers!" he said. He smiled and leaped up.

David's and my eyes grew so big I feared they would blow out their sockets.

"What should I say to them?" he asked Bowie.

"Oh no! Don't let them do it!" Bowie insisted. "RCA will rip them off!"

I quickly looked at Jimmy with heated confusion, seeking some advice, some thought of compromise, of finding a way.

"No, thanks," he said into the phone, and hung up.

I held my breath in disbelief. David dug his wrists into his eyes. It was hard to go against Bowie.

I learned later that Bowie had been in the middle of a huge legal battle with RCA. I think he was protecting us. He was the consummate businessman, above everything else, and I knew that about him. The Thin White Duke. Ziggy. The Man Who Fell to Earth. Human.

Fame puts you there where things are hollow (fame)
Fame, it's not your brain, it's just the flame
That burns your change to keep you insane (fame)[1]

The *Rashomon* Principle

PHILIP

In those days, I was drunkenly oblivious to the business side of things. (I still kind of am, though not drunkenly, thank God.) I had never even heard the story of Jimmy hanging up on the woman from RCA until one Christmas season, in the mid-2000s when Lori and I met up with David, and he told us the story. I don't remember having much feeling about it one way or another (heh-heh) except for thinking how insufferable and unpleasant Jimmy could be. (For the record, he could also be very cool, and he contributed a lot of good things to our recordings.) Stories like that seem apocryphal to me, even when they are true. If the Student Teachers never signed a major-label deal—and of course we did not—that wasn't the reason.

---

1   Lyrics from "Fame" by David Bowie, Carlos Alomar, and John Lennon, from David Bowie's *Young Americans*, 1975.

DAVID

Then there was the night, at Jimmy and Laura's, when a rep from RCA called with an offer. I was there, and so was David Bowie. A pretty heady evening, to say the least. Jimmy covered the phone and asked Bowie how he should respond to the offer . . . and on Bowie's advice he said no and hung up the phone. Despite the shock of the moment, I thought it was pretty cool that he had the balls to pass on an offer from a major label. And, even more so, that it was Bowie who told him not to let us sign with them. In my mind, it was just a matter of time before we would get a better deal with another label, anyway. It seemed like a bold strategy to turn away the crumbs in order to hold out for the loaf (as the saying goes). Or maybe it was just hubris. Either way, it was only well after the band broke up that the "RCA moment" stood out to me as a turning point in our trajectory . . . and it's impossible to imagine how our lives might have turned out had things gone any other way.

ANTONE

Sadly, the band never recorded a full-length album, due to our relationship with Jimmy Destri. He treated us like his children for whom he produced a single for Ork Records, that he brokered, and two tracks for the Marty Thau compilation, that he was also responsible for. Maybe we could have had an album for RCA or Modern, but he would have been the producer.

JOE

As I have only recently learned of Jimmy's RCA turndown, my delayed-by-thirty-seven-years reaction is "Gee, that's unfortunate, I would have loved the opportunity to put out a record on a major label." But that's it. There's way too much going on now in everyone's lives and worlds to get worked up about that.

LORI

Oh, RCA! Yes I'm with Philip on that one. I remember going up to the office and being shown the "Ashes to Ashes" video and how cool it was being there, and not as a fan trying to get a press kit or itinerary for another band. Instead we were invited to a bona fide record company as musicians. I don't remember turning down the offer to be signed; I simply remember being there. And I do recall it had something to do with David's mother.

. ● .

Disbanding

The Student Teachers continued to perform after I had left. They released an EP titled *Easter '78—Halloween '80*, in 1981, which they coproduced themselves with Antone and Jay Burnett. They decided to disband on Halloween 1980, exactly one year after our big Palladium show with Iggy. Elin Wilder noted in the *New York Rocker*: "Student Teachers have officially disbanded—spin-offs to come. . . ."[2]

---

2   Elin Wilder, "A Foot in Every Mouth," *New York Rocker*, January 1981, 14.

31

LOCUS

THERE WERE TWENTY-FOUR AISLES. I took a shopping cart from the front line and began in aisle 1. Milk. Eggs. American cheese. Swiss cheese. I looked farther down the aisle. There were at least fifteen more glass cabinets bursting with frozen boxes of pancakes and waffles and egg sandwiches and omelets. At the end of the aisle, I pushed the cart to the right. I looked over. No end in sight. Twenty-four aisles.

I turned up the next one. Bread. White. Ritz crackers. Pretzels. English muffins. Popcorn. Cheez Doodles. I pushed forward and swung around into the next aisle. Frozen foods. I saw some frozen pizza. It was small and simple. Just cheese. I had to get it. Jimmy loved pizza. And how could we order pizza out here? No one would deliver pizza so far out here—wherever this was. I grabbed the pizza and shut the door. I looked at the next refrigerator: French beans, peas, lima beans. I loved lima beans. I grabbed a box. I swung the cart around and wheeled forward up the next aisle, my eyelids drooping as the unending glass cases began to numb my brain. Who was all this for?

When I got back to the front I saw the twenty-four cash register stations—one for each aisle. There were lines of twenty people deep at each one, and they all had at least two carts filled with hundreds of dollars' worth of food. And enough kids with them to fill a football stadium.

I looked in my cart. Eight things. I pulled the money out of my pocket. Three hundred dollars. I was supposed to get more—a lot more. I looked across the interstellar expanse of the Staten Island Grand Union. What if I got lost? Would anyone ever find me?

In October—about a month after I last saw Bowie—Jimmy bought a house in Huguenot, Staten Island. Blondie's album, *Autoamerican*, was about to be released and Jimmy needed to invest his money a little more wisely. So, to the Staten Island tax shelter we relocated.

Before we left Jones Street, Jimmy arranged for the floors of the new house to be covered in wall-to-wall pink carpeting. Then he took me to the Upper East Side of Manhattan to a ritzy furniture showroom. Although I don't remember the name, it was so exclusive, it didn't have any signs out front—only a nondescript front door, as if it was a private house. When we entered, we were met by a gentleman who described himself as our "personal shopper" and said that he would be performing with us as we moved through the showrooms, focusing on all the choices. Performing? Who performs to sell a sofa? If ever I felt like a total fraud, it was in that buried and clandestine showroom. I just wanted to get out of there, and fast. Within ten minutes, I chose a white sectional sofa that came in dozens of tiny sections so you could set it up in any way you liked. I didn't care how it looked. I just wanted out. I smiled and thanked the personal shopper performance guy and pulled Jimmy out of there at lightning speed. It was all too surreal. I wanted to get back to real. Except I don't think I ever did.

Although it was clear Jimmy wanted to be near his family, the house he'd bought was so far out in Staten Island that it nearly crossed state lines, over into New Jersey. Even worse, the house was at the end of a dead-end street surrounded by hollow, soundless woods. Maybe it was my chaotic thinking at the time, but the space, the emptiness of that world, the lack of structure and tangible meaning, and the interminable silence, ripped me to near complete insanity. I was so lost.

When we finally moved in, there was just the couch and a television in the living room, the bed in the master bedroom, and our old dining room table in the kitchen. And that was it. Inside that three-thousand-square foot, four-bedroom house, that was it—no more furniture, and pink wall-to-wall carpeting. Spooky space outside and spooky space inside.

It's not that the loft where I grew up in SoHo was that undersized and intimate. But Manhattan was, and is, small and closely held together. I was raised in a world where all the space around me was filled—by buildings or people or garbage or taxicabs. I didn't understand open space or sparseness or the inevitable silence that inhabits those cavities. What I did understand was closeness and defenses and collaboration. That distant neighborhood was punctuated by unoccupied woods between the houses and it screamed remote isolation.

I was still supposed to rest. I'd been told to rest. Although it had been over six months since I was diagnosed with MS, I was still told to rest and not push myself too hard. That was the worst part of that whole diagnosis. I had to rest. I didn't know how to do that. And none of my friends or family knew how to do that. Work and pushing oneself was the only way I had learned to exist. And when we played, we always played hard.

Jimmy wasn't around much and that left me alone in the house. *Autoamerican* was released in November, but Blondie didn't seem to be touring to support it, although Debbie was appearing on *The Muppet Show* and *Saturday Night Live*, with Chris and Clem. But Jimmy wasn't with them. I didn't know what inter-band politics was happening between them, and I was pretty sure I didn't want to know. Jimmy was also involved in production work for other young bands, so that kept him away in Manhattan nearly all the time.

More and more, I found myself hiding in the walk-in closet in the master bedroom. The bedroom was near the size of our entire apartment on Jones Street and the closet occupied one corner. I spent most of my time inside that closet, sitting on the floor, with the door shut. Claustrophobia had no locus in there because it was a room in and of itself. I didn't have enough clothes to take up more than five hangers and a shelf, leaving me plenty of room. I stayed in there, watching a portable black-and-white Sony TV and reading.

I hated it.

It may have also been out of concern for my health that the Staten Island move was made, I don't know. But for some reason, it rang more unseemly to me. As if it was the beginning of the end—that in the interest of resting,

I was to be kept far away from the world, where my friends, family, and social life were, and in the interest of resting, I was to cook and clean and marry Jimmy and be something I wasn't. In the interest of resting.

One afternoon, I woke up late, and I turned and noticed that Jimmy was in bed next to me. It was surprising, because I hadn't seen him in four days. I sat up. I thought I might make pancakes, but when I swung my legs to the side of the bed to get up, I was suddenly pulled back down. I started to giggle, but when I looked up I saw fury in Jimmy's face. I tried to pull myself away but was immediately pulled down again.

"Jimmy! What are you doing?"

"We're having sex! Now!" he screamed.

I pulled away.

"Stop it!"

"We never have sex anymore!"

"You're never here, Jimmy! What are you doing?"

I jerked myself away harder, then jumped off the bed and ran downstairs. I sat on the sofa and pulled my knees up to my chest. My left thumb started shaking. I looked at it and put it under my butt. Jimmy ran down the stairs.

He came over to me and pulled me up.

"What are you doing?" I shouted. He tried to drag me back to the stairs, but I jerked away and marched to the phone in the kitchen.

"Who the hell are you calling? Your fucking boyfriend?!" he snapped.

"That's crazy! You're crazy!"

Suddenly he slapped my face and kicked me onto the floor. The phone flew out of my hand, but I swiftly stood up and grabbed it and dialed his parents. Jimmy threw up his hands and walked back upstairs.

About fifteen minutes later, Jimmy's dad drove up and came in the front door. He gave me a hug and told me to get a bag of clothes, that he was taking me home to my parents. Then he screamed for Jimmy to come down to the living room. When he did, I raced upstairs to throw some things in a bag, and I heard Jimmy's dad go ballistic on him.

When I returned to the stairs, the afternoon sun sliced through the windows and blinded me for a moment. I walked down and saw Jimmy sitting on the sofa, his head in his hands and his dad standing over him. When I reached the bottom, Jimmy's dad started to walk me out to his car, and as he did, he snapped at Jimmy, "Never, ever hit a woman, young man! Do you understand me?!"

I climbed into the passenger seat and Jimmy's dad got in and turned on the car. As we backed out of the driveway, Jimmy stood in the doorway and watched us. He looked so lost and broken, as if he had been awake for the last month with no sleep, or a break, or even water. His face was falling to the ground, silver and bony. He was a used coin sitting on the train tracks waiting to be run over. The cocaine was eating him alive. My heart wrenched itself. He needed help. But I wasn't it.

As his father pulled out of the driveway I watched Jimmy turn away and shut the door to the house. A painful burning started racing inside my legs.

32

EAR INN

THE PHONE RANG. JANE PICKED IT UP, then turned to me.

"It's for you," she said.

I took the receiver.

"Hello?"

"I've had an accident! I'm over on Spring Street by the river! The car's totaled!"

It was Jimmy.

"I'm bleeding!"

"What happened?" I asked.

"Come get me. Can you come get me?" he begged.

It was early 1981 and Jimmy had crashed his car a few blocks from my parents' loft in SoHo. We had broken up after his father had brought me home a few weeks previously, because I didn't want to be in the relationship anymore. I wasn't sure what I wanted, but I knew I didn't want to be left abandoned way out in Staten Island anymore. I hadn't seen Jimmy for a few weeks, and he wasn't too pleased with the whole separation thing.

I met him at the Ear Inn on Spring Street near the Hudson River. He was sitting at the bar. The bartender had given him a napkin for the blood streaming out of his nose. He seemed okay, though a bit beaten up, like he had been up all night again. I took him home and he crashed in my loft bed. We decided to talk about things in a few days. Maybe it all could be salvaged.

Jimmy had moved out of Huguenot and into a duplex in the West Village. The place was on the first floor, looking out over a park. It had a twisting staircase to the second floor and a beautifully ornate fireplace in the master bedroom. There was a small kitchen in the back, with a window in the wall facing the living room and a full dining room next to it, with brass candelabra on the table. Another different world, but closer to my SoHo home. We got back together and I moved into the duplex with him.

It had been nearly a year since I'd been diagnosed, and I was still living in between myself. Jimmy was gone all of the time, either in the recording studio doing production work or in all-night manic sessions composing on the synthesizer in the living room. Then he was dead asleep all day. And the single common thread: cocaine. It was still there. It was everywhere. He didn't seem to know that I was aware of it, either.

Even though Jimmy and I had a number of heart-to-hearts about how the drugs had to end, I knew the coke would never really go away. It wasn't just that I had stopped it since before the diagnosis, which set up a wall of a separate life between us—it's that it was killing him, and that scared me. I could see the breakdown of his body as it got progressively thinner, his skin getting painfully dry, his eyes sinking into big black orbs of drug-induced capsules in his head. I saw it happening.

Just like with alcohol, drugs were and are a fundamental element in the rock 'n' roll structure. It's always felt like the soaring ivory tower of rock music can't stand on its own two legs without the support that drugs provide. When I think about it, it's not just that the world where rock subsists is at night, after the hours when nine-to-fivers punch the clock and close their briefcases—though it helps, due to the underlying web of nighttime crawlers and after-hours "shadowers" who bring that world to life. Dark. Discreet. Illegal. Immoral. But, in actuality, it always seemed that, in order to make the rock 'n' roll machine churn, drugs had to be there. They seemed to create an environment that boosted vast creativity. It blasted down those cement walls that exist only in a clear cognitive state. I saw it in Jimmy and in many people—the drugs inspired those moments of visionary inspiration and mind-bending brainstorms to come alive. The problem was the side effect, which was too often death.

Although I never got so high I lost consciousness, like those taking heroin or heavy quaaludes, doing so was and is extremely common. Drug dealers swim at night, rock 'n' roll thrives at night, and that's the tenor of revolt one experiences at that moment—taking drugs isn't a wholly aberrant act in that world: It makes sense. It's going to the ATM to get cash or to the dentist for a filling or adding oregano to the pasta sauce. It's what's done, it's normal. It's convention.

Many of us in rock 'n' roll—stars and not—have borne the scourge of drugs and alcohol. Too many—Hendrix, Joplin, Sid Vicious, Johnny Thunders, Dee Dee Ramone, Amy Winehouse, Michael Jackson— have died, and many more still must manage the long-term aftereffects and demands of previous drug addiction today. Most of the Student Teachers and Blondie were knocked down by it—Chris Stein almost died when cocaine addiction caused an underlying disease to blow up, nearly killing him. Bowie and Iggy Pop were in and out of rehab throughout their lives. Many of us have survived, but at a cost. And it begs a disconcerting question: Can art—great art—only come to life within a pool of suffering? Is art only pain?

The thing was, in that duplex apartment in early '81, I saw cocaine continue to destroy Jimmy, even though it energized his imagination. Even worse, there were moments when the coke-fueled mania sparked his anger. The anger didn't go after me when we were in the West Village, but it certainly could, because in the past, it had.

Again, like when we were back in Huguenot, our opposing schedules found us not seeing each other much. I started taking acting classes at the Lee Strasberg Theatre Institute. I'm not sure why, but I felt I needed to get out, away from what I knew, away from Jimmy.

In August of '81, Alice Cooper played the Savoy. Jimmy was out of town, on Blondie business, and I decided to swing uptown to see Alice. Oddly, I went alone. I had never done that before and I wasn't sure why I decided to do so then. The club was packed. It was Cooper's Special Forces tour and he was in top form. I watched him cranking in with "I'm Eighteen" and "Under My Wheels," and it sounded great. But I didn't shout or dance or jump to see him better. I just wandered through the club, hearing him but not really watching him. I kept gazing around, looking for someone I knew, a friend—something, anything.

Finally, I stopped and looked carefully around me at the flashing lights inside the darkened club and the frantically painted and bedazzled Alice Cooper fans, and for some reason I suddenly thought of John Lennon. He had been dead for nearly nine months then, and his death had rattled not just the city, not just the rock 'n' roll world, but everyone. It wasn't just that a crazed fan got so mentally sidelined that he felt the crushing need to kill our idol, it was the fact that our idol had died—that he was actually human despite all our—my—certainty that he wasn't.

A dreary sadness grew inside me and I recognized what my problem was: this world. I realized, as Alice Cooper's stage lights circled furiously through the audience, that it was fake, a sham, counterfeit, a pure illusion. It was not genuine—meaning, it was not genuine for me. And it was holding me inside a time machine of indefiniteness. I needed to know which way was up and which way was down. And I needed it to stay that way every day. I needed to know that when I shut the door to go out, when I came back, everything would be the same as when I'd left it—at least for the time being. The chaos had become too dominant. It controlled everything. I needed it to be stopped. At that moment, I needed that. I needed to grow up.

It was finished. All of it was finished. The music, the dancing, the drugs, the never-ending apartments, the touring, the endless late nights—and Jimmy—it was finished.

It didn't feel like a needed or remarkable relief. It felt more like an absolute. It was impossible not to end it all.

. . .

THE FOLLOWING WEEK, WHILE JIMMY WAS OUT OF TOWN, I called Jane, and she came over with a big empty suitcase. She helped me pack up everything that was inside the apartment; then we went outside, hailed a cab, and I went home.

Jimmy found out about it when he returned from work at the end of the week. He called and we talked and he called and we talked. And then he stopped calling.

"Of her memories, most were happy."
—*Mrs. Dalloway*, by Virginia Woolf

33

DIVESTITURE

THE YEAR I LEFT JIMMY, I started at NYU, studying writing. Eventually, I got married, earned a law degree, and had two daughters. I finally read up on multiple sclerosis and learned a lot about it. Unfortunately, starting when I was twenty-two years old, I began having many exacerbations—I even lost a semester at college due to it.

Five years after I had been diagnosed, I joined an experimental medication study at Rockefeller University with Dr. Herman Weinreb, where one of the other participants died during the course of the study. She hadn't had the condition much longer than me. That was an eye-opener. But as I grew more aware and became more proactive, I learned that the key to MS is time. Even more critically, the disease affects every single person differently. Again, I was lucky. After my many exacerbations, I always got back on my feet, after rest and medication.

Then, not long after my youngest daughter started kindergarten, I completely lost my ability to walk. Twenty years after I was diagnosed.

Yes, that woman I saw when I was fifteen, being pushed in the wheelchair, down Seventh Avenue, and how awful I thought it would be to live in a wheelchair—her life became my life. But I was sorely wrong about one thing—it was not awful—far from it.

What I learned, rather, was that we all have mountains to surmount—drug addiction, the loss of a loved one, learning disabilities, the inability to walk or to see. The challenge lies in whether you allow that mountain to crush you, or whether you scale and conquer it, which means making it work for you, not against you. Yes, some of us have more control than others, but really, none of us has any true control. I realized, after I started college, that no matter what, we can't control what happens to us, but we can control how we react to it.

To that end, I've often thought about why I didn't just leave Jimmy after the first time he hit me. Part of it, certainly, was my young age; part of it was my confused belief that a woman needs to be with a man to be complete and accepted; part of it was the misconception that life with a rock star—any star—is the only life worth living, and of course there was the delusional state drugs kept me in. Thankfully, I figured out how wrong those beliefs were and said goodbye.

Nonetheless, if there was one thing I learned from that intense, exquisite life in rock 'n' roll, the chance to be a drummer for the Student Teachers, and the gift I was given in knowing Bowie and all the Blondies, it was that it all doesn't end there. It doesn't end with the last note of the song, or the last clapping fan in the front row as the theater closes, or the final step you are physically able to take across the street. It continues— because it's always time to move on to the next challenge. That's exactly what I did, and still do. So I'm still lucky.

REDEPLOYED

BILL ARNING

Forming a rock band in my late teen years seemed a very natural activity for a music-obsessed youth like me. I had absorbed my older sister's music tastes for the Doors and the Velvet Underground, rather than my brother's liking for more mainstream acts such as the Beatles, Stones, and Allman Brothers. I also had a taste for all things avant-garde, from John Cage to Andy Warhol. I loved the music I was hearing before I ever found my way to CBGB. I saw the Talking Heads for the first time in the safe environment of the Kitchen art space on Broome Street. When Laura and I became friends, I was very intoxicated by the heady artistic atmosphere at her father Doug Davis's Wooster Street loft, and seeing works by Sturtevant, Robert Rauschenberg, Nam June Paik, and Komar and Melamid left a profound impression of wild sophistication compared to my parents' tame Picasso and Matisse posters. Only years later did I learn that, as the Talking Heads sang, early punk in New York was also, surprisingly, a field dominated by "artists only"—or at least art students—and that most of my colleagues of my later career in contemporary art, who are near my age, were also seeing, or usually playing in, the same bands I was listening to.

CBGB was also my stage for coming out as a gay man and was where I developed a disdain for gay mainstream tastes in music that lingers, to some degree, to this day. (While I have no interest in Lady Gaga, I did in the last ten years develop an unhealthy obsession with opera, which is a place a lot of ex–punk rockers spend their early dotage, since opera and punk share a desublimated tendency toward overexpressed emotions.) As this book makes clear, my obsession with the very out figure of Lance Loud—especially with his ties to Andy Warhol and *Interview* magazine—taught me how be a gay man in both positive and negative ways. I knew I would hate being in an all-male straight rock band and the Students Teachers' mix of gay men, women, and charmingly ambiguous heterosexual men was a perfect platform for me, one that seems wildly ahead of its time.

TODAY: *Bill is executive director at Contemporary Arts Museum Houston.*

LORI REESE

Sometime around 1977, my friend Michael Alago and I went into a record store in Brooklyn. When I slapped what I'd found in the bins onto the counter up front, the man at the register offered me a job. I was sixteen and confused by my own inner stirrings, and it was there, in Borough Park, Brooklyn (of all places), that my burgeoning otherness was confirmed and embraced. And that's how it was on the music scene in New York City in the late 1970s. Bill, Philip, David, Laura, and I, a haphazard collection of teenage individuals, became enduring friends who discovered we had the foundation of a band. No matter how short-lived and contentious that union may have been, it is partially due to its murky cohesion that a book has now been completed.

When the Student Teachers recorded our first single, we were not making a holiday cake, nope; we were making a record, and that was all that mattered. No amount of drugs, cakes, or boys could be better than that. That moment was critical; it was palpable, visceral. My dreams had become my reality. The process of recording at that time, and in that studio—a studio where bands I most admired had made records in the past—was the pinnacle. Making a record was so cool, so super cool, and (probably to the detriment of all those around me) the finished product was not as significant as the experience. The end product would represent completion; the activity would cease and that would suck.

Similar to the Patti Smith, *Live at the Ocean Club*, and Sparks bootlegs I discovered at that record store so many decades ago in Brooklyn, the happenstance of our unique characters, which combined positively when we met at Max's Kansas City and CBGB, resulted in the Student Teachers. Although just a small part of Laura Davis's memoir, that band was an essential element of her personal history. Thanks to *The Girl in the Back*, she makes us remember that, yeah, it was great, and, yes, we did make a band. Bands break up, but memories continue. I was in it for the experience, and I wouldn't have had it happen any other way.

TODAY: *Lori is director of archive sales at Redux Pictures.*

JODY ROBELO-KATZ

The late '70s were an amazing time to be growing up in New York City, loving all types of music and being able to be different and completely accepted, which brought so many of us together at CBGB and Max's.

We were all at many of the same shows, and through mutual friends, I met Lori Reese, who introduced me to the rest of the Student Teachers. They were all so smart, funny, and unique. They took me in right away, and I helped out where I could—lugging equipment, then booking shows and doing whatever else an eighteen-year-old manager could do.

Though the events were the same for everyone, our experiences were different. This is Laura's story—it's the story of the girl set up behind everyone else on the stage, playing really hard on those pink drums, who was so much more than the girl in the back.

TODAY: *Jody is a travel agent specializing in booking tours for bands.*

DAVID SCHARFF

The five of us, along with the life support of Jody and Antone . . . and, later, our friend Joe . . . converged in downtown New York City in a space free of adult supervision and filled with excitement and possibilities. We were seeing all of the incredible bands playing at the time—from the already famous Patti Smith and Ramones, to the obscure but brilliant Mumps and Erasers—at tiny clubs like CBGB and Max's. We loved our bands! Seeing them whenever and wherever they played—and being able to stand next to them in the audience at each other's gigs—became the thing I most looked forward to. We were teenagers at a big ongoing party with an amazing constellation of older (how ancient twenty-five seemed at the time!) brilliant stars-in-the-making, and our love for them bound us together. Just being fans in that scene was electrifying. It felt like a kind of privilege to be a part of it. So it wasn't long before we made the move from fandom to "band-dom" . . . and became the Student Teachers.

When we played, it felt to me like the most natural thing in the world to do. I loved the role [of front man] and played it to the hilt. Our teenage charm and hooky original songs won us fans, got us opening spots with the bands we followed and adored, and eventually drew the attention of Jimmy Destri. He took us on as his special project. He wanted to become a producer, and we were his poppy young guinea pigs. We quickly found ourselves recording our songs . . . putting out singles on Ork and Red Star . . . headlining weekends at CBGB, Max's, Hurrah. . . . It felt like our momentum was unstoppable!

The part of the story when we didn't sign with RCA, however, was not the defining moment of the life of the band. The drama of being a teenager on the stages of CBGB, Max's, the Palladium—of opening for the likes of Iggy Pop, Richard Hell, the Cramps—that was what defined it for me. We were living out a teenage rock star fantasy.

As happens with most fantasies, that one didn't fully materialize, but the stories from that time are so much fun to tell! They're also fun to read, and reading Laura's stories brings me right back to the exhilarating and heartrending moments we shared.

TODAY: *David is senior manager of creative services and special projects at the Annenberg Foundation.*

JOE KATZ

I was a late arrival to the Student Teachers' endless party, joining about eighteen months after the band's inception. I was playing bass in the Mumps, one of the STs' "big brother and/or sister" bands, and, through circumstances I can't recall, started sitting in (as the jazz folk say) on guitar with the STs at a couple gigs. That eventually led to an offer to join full-time as the second (or "other") guitarist—again, I don't remember if they asked or I begged (probably B), but there I was. Maybe, as there was the strong Blondie connection, they decided they needed their own Frank Infante, which makes me the Frank Infante of the new wave, except the new wave already had a Frank Infante.

I am very, very grateful to have lived through and participated in the New York punk wave happening. It was really the most fun one could have, and we had it. The best people, the best times. The two most important life lessons I received from being in bands are: most amps shouldn't be carried by just one person, and don't always believe what people tell you.

I had a mostly wonderful time for the year I was in the band, and got the chance to play some truly great songs with even greater people who I'm happy to say are still my friends. I hope.

TODAY: *Joe is a retired hockey coach and a big fan of George Sanders.*

ANTONE DESANTIS

My introduction to the Student Teachers came via Lori, when she was a clerk at my local Brooklyn record shop, turning me on to obscure punk singles and rare concert bootlegs. She told me about her band and her punk name, which was Z. B. Stripe. In April of '78 she invited me to see the Teachers play at CBGB.

Since I had a car, I drove Lori/Z. B. to and from the show, so she put me on the band's guest list. After the show ended, I was standing in front of the club, watching some of the band members attempt to hail taxis to different parts of Manhattan with their gear. I volunteered to drive them to their respective spaces and quickly became the band's official roadie. I soon found myself surrounded by a whole new set of friends and obsessive music fans. Many of them lived in parts of the metro New York City area (like Larchmont) that seemed so foreign compared to my Brooklyn neighborhood. They were an eclectic bunch of freaks and geeks, some bearing witty fictitious punk names, wearing outlandish attire with multicolor dyed hair. While many of my childhood Brooklyn buddies were living the *Saturday Night Fever* lifestyle, disco dancing at nightspots like Studio 54 and Xenon, I was hanging with this motley gang, cultivating the second wave of New York City punk at CBGB and Max's. My connection to the Student Teachers gave me a permanent slot on the guest list of both clubs, allowing me to see countless esoteric artists and listen to a wide array of groundbreaking new music nightly. Working for the band led me to drive around equipment for the Cramps, the Mumps, the Know, the Speedies, and other area bands, and after hanging around until the clubs closed at 3 a.m., the bands would pay me for moving their gear! When that was done, we'd go to Bill's for after-show breakfast parties. We were celebrating our wild youths.

After Laura was asked to leave the band, Jody funded the band's last recording and the remaining members gave me a vote of confidence as co–record producer with the band with Jay Burnett. At the time, I was going to the New School for audio engineering, planning to be a record producer in the music industry. I was inspired by Jimmy, by watching him work with the band in the studio for both the Ork and Red Star recordings. Besides, he and his sister Donna grew up within ten blocks of me, and he and I had attended the same Catholic grade school as kids. After the band broke up, all that experience led me to continue working with bands as a booking agent; with Joe in the Swinging Madisons; and with Philip in the Nightmares. Eventually, I gave that all up and found myself in a "real" music biz job working as a sales and marketing representative for various record labels and distribution companies, which is where I continue to work today.

I was fortunate to be a part of the Student Teachers' crew during my formative years. It was thirty months of learning so much about life, music, and the business. Although I should have been in college during that time period instead, I, and so many others, got an education from the Student Teachers. Along the way, the band helped me discover so much music and develop innumerable relationships, and taught me lifelong lessons that I will cherish forever. It was the most thrilling time of my life.

TODAY: *Antone is a music sales and marketing manager.*

PHILIP SHELLEY

I was sixteen years old when the Student Teachers were formed. A group of us from Larchmont had been going to CBGB regularly for a couple of years, but Laura was my first "New York girlfriend" (to quote Jonathan Richman, at whose NYU concert in the fall of 1977 Bill asked David and me to join his nascent band).

In between Student Teachers activities, Laura and I did a lot of regular dopey teenage stuff like hanging out at her babysitting job in the West Village, or holding hands at the movies, or getting ice cream at the variety store on (then desolate) Spring St. I remember being scared of her father, amused by her little sister, and grateful for the understanding of her youngish stepmother, who was "cool." When Laura ended up with Jimmy, I was furious, as only a teenager can be, but I made sure to get a good song out of it. ("Drop Your Name," now lost to time, which featured a completely psychotic synthesizer solo from Bill.)

When I think about the Student Teachers, I dwell less on the messy, protracted crack-up than on the rather innocent and earnest spirit that initially drew us together—all of us so young and so deliriously in love with music and its magical transformational properties. The bonds we formed then have proved to be incredibly resilient, even into middle age— the experience was simply too mutually formative for it to be otherwise. I learned so much from the other Student Teachers, it's ridiculous—and I continue to learn from them.

From our current cultural vantage point, it seems almost unimaginable that there once existed a world where art was of central, calamitous importance, untethered to capital or institutions; where it was acknowledged that creative exploration involved a certain amount of existential risk and danger; and where money scarcely mattered because everything was cheap and took place outside (or beneath) the notice of the mainstream—including parents and the police. And, even more unbelievably, there were entire neighborhoods devoted to this ethos! I think the Student Teachers were extremely fortunate to come of age in a time and place like that, where we were able to learn about ourselves and the world we lived in through songs and art, and in the communities that coalesced around music-making and writing and performance and every other flavor of artistic practice.

I have gotten older and the world has changed profoundly, but the lessons I learned and the values I internalized during that relatively brief window of time were foundational to me, and if I have not always been true to them, they still constitute my default angle of engagement with the world.

TODAY: *Philip is a writer, editor, and community organizer in Portland, Maine. He still performs occasionally and writes songs with his longtime musical partner, Amanda Thorpe.*

PAUL RUTNER (DRUMMER OF THE MUMPS)

I was knocking around playing in cover bands on Long Island when I met some people who were in the burgeoning New York City music scene. They were making original music, playing the clubs in Manhattan; Mother's, Max's and CBGB. They told tales of a band that played a set of twelve songs in less than twenty minutes! I was intrigued and ventured forth. The first time I went to CB's, I saw a lanky figure with stringy black hair, skinny Levi's, and black leather jacket. Patti Smith! I thought to myself, That is one ugly woman! It turned out that it was actually Joey Ramone.

One thing led to another, and I ended up auditioning for and getting in to the Mumps. The first date that was scheduled for us was at Max's Kansas City, playing with Cherry Vanilla. I was nervous as hell. I had only even been to Max's a couple of times before and had for years heard that it was the foremost bastion of underground New York hipness and decadence. For a middle-class suburban kid, visions of the Velvet Underground, heroin, and people much, much cooler than I flooded my mind. It was a long way from my hometown of Levittown, New York.

That night and gig started a long roller-coaster ride that yielded years of fun, triumph, disappointment, romance, love, heartbreak, missed opportunities, grasped opportunities, friendships, feuds, laughs, and tears. The New York City scene in the late '70s and early '80s was an incubator for a culture that spread throughout the U.S. and beyond. It helped shape my life, and it was an honor to be a part of that time and place. I forged many lasting lifelong friendships in the course of that era (Joe Katz was the best man at my wedding, for instance). And . . . oh, what stories have been told, when we are fortunate enough to see each other again and reconnect.

Laura's book, and reconnecting with her after a disconnect that lasted more than thirty years, has helped rekindle many of the feelings, both good and bad, that permeated the scene, and my life, during those band years. The funny thing is that I reconnected with Laura only a few years ago, when I read an interview with the Student Teachers, in conjunction with the release of a retrospective CD of their recordings, and she revealed, in the interview, that she had been kicked out of her house partially because of her dalliance with me, one night, so long ago. I had not known that for all that time. Obviously, I had to contact her, at that point.

TODAY: *Paul is married, with two great kids (both of whom have stayed with Laura, in New York, when visiting there), living in Austin, Texas, and works for a nonprofit educational association. He is the founder and principal stockholder of Notary Sojac, LLC.*

THE REMAINING MEMBERS OF THE MUMPS

- Kristian Hoffman is musical director for the magic/vaudeville club Brookledge Follies in Los Angeles, tours with and writes songs for Prince Poppycock, and is a weekly DJ at LuxuriaMusic.com.
- Rob Duprey lives in Baltimore, and is married, with two teenage kids, Fiona and Liam. He is in a band with some friends he used to play with when he was fourteen years old: The group gigs around DC and Baltimore.
- Kevin Kiely passed away in 1997 after a long illness.
- Lance Loud passed away in 2001 from liver cancer.

BLONDIE

- The band is actively touring: Their latest CD, *Pollinator*, was released in summer 2017.
- Jimmy Destri eventually left Blondie to continue his work in songwriting, performing, and production with his own band the Sound Grenade. He is also currently a credentialed substance abuse therapist.

POSSIBLY, HOPEFULLY, MAYBE, VERY GOOD STUFF

WEBSITES

Laura Davis-Chanin: www.laurakdc.com
Bill Arning: www.camh.org
David Scharff: www.annenberg.org
Kristian Hoffman: www.luxuriamusic.com
Student Teachers: www.thestudentteachers.com

PODCASTS

Laura Davis-Chanin: *Phi Fic: A Fiction Podcast*

ALBUMS

The Student Teachers: *Invitation to the Student Teachers* on Nacional
    Records.
The Mumps: *How I Saved the World* on Sympathy for the Record Industry.
Blondie: *Pollinator* on BMG Records.
David Bowie: *Blackstar* on Sony Records.

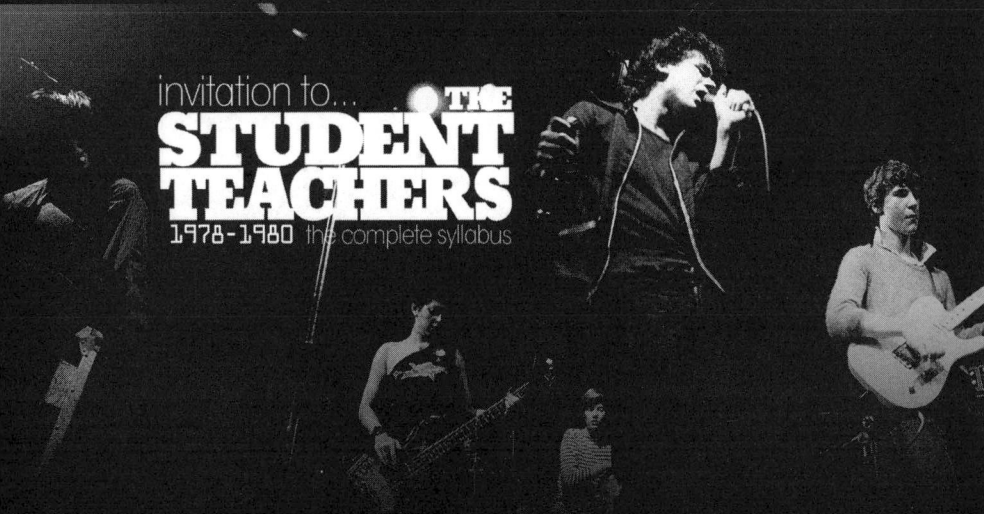

invitation to... **THE STUDENT TEACHERS**

1978-1980 the complete syllabus

"Love the Student Teachers. That's the real stuff, from the real, dirty, weird New York of yesteryear. The song 'Looks' breaks my heart in seventeen places every time I hear it."
Mike Doughty (Soul Coughing)

"That the Student Teachers didn't get an album deal was a miss on the part of the record companies. For a band of 16 and 17 year olds to have gone from being fans to a warm-up act to headliners within 2 years was itself impressive; and of course, like all the CB's bands, they wrote their own material and sounded like nobody else. "
Danny Fields

01. **CHRISTMAS WEATHER** - ORK Records — 1978
02. **CHANNEL THIRTEEN** - ORK Records — 1978
03. **WHAT I CAN'T FEEL** - Red Star Records, "2x5" — 1979
04. **LOOKS** - Red Star Records, "2x5" — 1979
05. **SECOND BEFORE** - Unreleased — 1979
06. **INVITATION TO...** - Self-Released — 1980
07. **SAMANTHA** - Self-Released — 1980
08. **CHRISTINA** - Self-Released — 1980
09. **PAST TENSE** - Self-Released — 1980

Available on CD
UPC - 753182545684
NCL20108

Available on LP from
Rave Up/Backstreet One Records
BAC17

 **NACIONAL** RECORDS

nacionalrecords.com